# HO[W T]O
## PROTECT
# book-
# stores
## AND WHY

# HOW TO PROTECT

# book-
# stores
# AND WHY

THE **Present** AND **Future** OF **Bookselling**

## DANNY CAINE

**Microcosm Publishing**
Portland, Ore | Cleveland, Ohio

*How to Protect Bookstores and Why: The Present and Future of Bookselling*

© Danny Caine, 2023

This edition © Microcosm Publishing, 2023

First edition, 5,000 copies, first published September 19, 2023

Book design by Joe Biel

ISBN 9781648411632

This is Microcosm #775

For a catalog, write or visit:

Microcosm Publishing

2752 N Williams Ave.

Portland, OR 97227

(503)799-2698

www.Microcosm.Pub/ProtectBookstores

Did you know that you can buy our books directly from us at sliding scale rates? Support a small, independent publisher and pay less than Amazon's price at **www.Microcosm.Pub**

*To join the ranks of high-class stores that feature Microcosm titles, talk to your rep:* In the U.S. **Como** (Atlantic), **Abraham** (Midwest), **Third Act** (Texas, Oklahoma, Louisiana, Arkansas), **Imprint** (Pacific), **Turnaround** in Europe, **Manda/UTP** in Canada, **New South** in Australia, and **GPS** in Asia, India, Africa, and South America.We are sold in the gift market by **Faire** and **Emerald**.

Library of Congress Cataloging-in-Publication Data

Names: Caine, Danny, author.
Title: How to protect bookstores and why : the present and future of
    bookselling / Danny Caine.
Description: Portland : Microcosm Publishing, [2023] | Includes
    bibliographical references. | Summary: "As bastions of culture, anchors
    of local retail districts, community gathering places, and the sources
    of new ideas, inspiration, and delight, bookstores have the capacity to
    save the world. Therefore, we need to protect them and the critical
    roles they fill in our communities. Danny Caine makes a compelling case
    for the power of small, local businesses in this thoughtful examination
    of the dynamic world of bookstores"-- Provided by publisher.
Identifiers: LCCN 2023013482 | ISBN 9781648411632 (trade paperback)
Subjects: LCSH: Booksellers and bookselling--United States. | Independent
    bookstores--United States. | Small business--United States.
Classification: LCC Z471 .C35 2023 | DDC 381/.45002--dc23/eng/20230513
LC record available at https://lccn.loc.gov/2023013482

# MICROCOSM · PUBLISHING

# ABOUT THE PUBLISHER

**Microcosm Publishing** is Portland's most diversified publishing house and distributor, with a focus on the colorful, authentic, and empowering. Our books and zines have put your power in your hands since 1996, equipping readers to make positive changes in their lives and in the world around them. Microcosm emphasizes skill-building, showing hidden histories, and fostering creativity through challenging conventional publishing wisdom with books and bookettes about DIY skills, food, bicycling, gender, self-care, and social justice. What was once a distro and record label started by Joe Biel in a drafty bedroom was determined to be *Publishers Weekly*'s fastest-growing publisher of 2022 and #3 in 2023, and is now among the oldest independent publishing houses in Portland, OR, and Cleveland, OH. We are a politically moderate, centrist publisher in a world that has inched to the right for the past 80 years.

Global labor conditions are bad, and our roots in industrial Cleveland in the '70s and '80s made us appreciate the need to treat workers right. Therefore, our books are MADE IN THE USA.

# CONTENTS

Introduction: Looking for Answers • 11

Chapter 1: "Layers of Community"
BIRCHBARK BOOKS & NATIVE ARTS, MINNEAPOLIS,
   MN • 25

Chapter 2: "We Just Figure Out How to Make
   It Work"
AVID BOOKSHOP, ATHENS, GA • 45

Chapter 3: "Opening the Doors More"
A ROOM OF ONE'S OWN, MADISON, WI • 63

Chapter 4: "This Accumulation of Histories"
SHAKESPEARE AND COMPANY, PARIS, FR • 81

Chapter 5: "How to Turn Information into a
   Weapon in the Fight for a Better World"
RED EMMA'S BOOKSTORE COFFEEHOUSE, BALTIMORE,
   MD • 101

Chapter 6: "A New Battle Every Year"
BOOKENDS & BEGINNINGS, EVANSTON, IL • 117

Chapter 7: "Can't Revolutionize from a
U-Haul Truck"
SEMICOLON BOOKSTORE & GALLERY, CHICAGO, IL •
133

Chapter 8: "I Can't Pretend We're Neutral
Anymore"
MOON PALACE BOOKS, MINNEAPOLIS, MN • 145

Chapter 9: "Nothing of Any Value Has Come
from a Place Like This"
TWO DOLLAR RADIO HEADQUARTERS, COLUMBUS,
OH, AND BIBLIOASIS BOOKSHOP, WINDSOR, ON
•157

Chapter 10: "You Cannot Dream Your Way
Out of Things Alone"
LOYALTY BOOKSTORES, WASHINGTON, DC • 175

Chapter 11: "The Community Is People"
SOURCE BOOKSELLERS, DETROIT, MI • 193

Conclusion: Finding More Questions • 205

In memory of

George Whitman

and

Lawrence Ferlinghetti

# INTRODUCTION:
# LOOKING FOR ANSWERS

*D*o bookstores even need to be protected? I can easily imagine some bookstore owners or workers saying no. After all, a bookstore, a for-profit business, doesn't need protection in the same way that, say, civil rights do. A business must figure out how to make money to stay open, so if a bookstore fails, that seems like a business problem, not a social, political, or cultural problem. We're talking stores, not museums. Right? On top of that, lots of bookstores aren't failing at all. By many indicators, the number of bookstores in America is increasing. Some people have even suggested that America is in the midst of an indie bookstore renaissance. If that's the case, why worry about protecting bookstores?

This is a great question, and one that this book sets out to answer. To do this, though, I first need to break it down into two separate questions: Why are bookstores *worth* protecting? And why do bookstores *need* protecting?

## WHY ARE BOOKSTORES *WORTH* PROTECTING?

To start, a bookstore's value resides in the benefits it provides to its community. Bookstores provide economic benefits in the same way that any independently owned retail business does: a central district with several thriving small businesses is an economic boon to any city. Such concentration of small businesses draws tourists, locals, and workers who spend and earn money that's more likely to stay local. According to a 2022 report by the American Booksellers Association, "Independent businesses provide [their] communities with substantial, quantifiable economic benefits relative to their chain competitors" as they "distribute profits to local ownership, employ a variety of personnel that might otherwise reside at a distant corporate office, routinely purchase goods and services from other local businesses, and generously support local charitable causes."[1] Bookstores are no exception: the ABA report claims that "approximately 29% of all revenue at independent bookstores immediately recirculates in the local economy. This translates to a local impact advantage of 109% that of chain competitor Barnes & Noble, and a massive 405% local impact advantage over Amazon."[2]

But when it comes to leading the charge in generating sustainable economic activity for a city or community, bookstores have unique advantages over other locally owned small businesses. According to a major report by the UK's Institute of Place Management, bookstores in particular "significantly contribute to the vitality and viability of their high streets."[3] They do this in myriad ways, from hosting events to providing jobs to helping surprise readers with new material. Many of these will be explored in the pages to come. But, crucially, bookstores have a way of lifting up other Main Street businesses: the Institute of Place Management claims, "The presence of bookshops can be expected to support wider high street activity, helping to prevent urban decay, increase or maintain property values and provide footfall for neighbouring businesses."[4]

Economics aside, bookstores also have cultural value that is worth protecting. They are powerful machines for uplifting, celebrating, discovering, and ultimately selling good books. There's still no match for a human bookseller in connecting the right book with the right reader; in fact, it's one of the literary world's great pleasures to be in the capable service of a talented bookseller. My friend Jeff Deutsch, director of Chicago's

Seminary Co-op Bookstores, has long spoken eloquently and passionately about the cultural value of what he calls "good bookstores." In his 2022 book, *In Praise of Good Bookstores*, Deutsch writes that "good bookstores are a repository for great books and a testing ground for recently published aspirants to greatness."[5] In Deutsch's view, booksellers are "providing great cultural labor, these transcendental readers, these professors of books."[6] It can be argued that this is one of the most important jobs of the bookseller: to find and promote and love the books that are good, that do good in this world. The groundbreaking books, the books that tell important stories, the books that see and elevate historically marginalized people. Amazon doesn't care about this work; they see books as mere objects in their massive data-collecting flywheel machine. This also seems increasingly true of the so-called "Big Five" publishers: Penguin Random House, HarperCollins, Hachette, Macmillan, and Simon & Schuster. It certainly looks like these publishers have lately given their attention (and marketing dollars) to blockbusters. If the biggest makers and sellers of books are focusing on books that will simply make the most money, who is left to advocate for the offbeat, the groundbreaking, the dare-I-say *important?* Booksellers. Bookstores. Bookstores are crucial in creating a world of books beyond those that appear on Walmart's shelves; for this reason, bookstores are worth protecting.

In addition to connecting readers with new or groundbreaking books, bookstores can also introduce members of their communities to social movements. There's a rich history of radical, activist, and feminist bookstores that serve as a durable entry point into political engagement. In this way, a bookstore is actually more than space facilitating the exchange of goods for money. As Kimberly Kinder writes in her book *The Radical Bookstore: Counterspace for Social Movements*, "Activists operating bookstores and infoshops rarely maintain single-use storefronts. Instead, they treat the space as an enabling resource sustaining many functions through continual repurposing."[7] Selling books is a function of these bookstores, yes, but so are lots of other things. A crucial element of bookstores is permanence: while a protest can last a few hours, a radical bookstore can last decades. Kinder calls radical bookstores "constructed spaces that find a home in retail and that leverage the durability and porosity of retail to advance political causes"; as she writes, "Having autonomous space, instead of relying only on seized or borrowed space, constructs additional opportunities for organizing."[8] Because bookstores are permanent or semi-permanent spaces, activists can easily use them to advance their causes and welcome new activists into the fold. Viewed in this context, the bookstore is no longer simply a cute place to buy books; it's an incubator for activists and changemakers. As Kinder explains, "The point of constructing radical bookstores and libraries is not to make quaint community spaces. On the contrary, the point is to challenge capitalism, imperialism, white privilege, patriarchy, and homophobia in a significant way that poses material threats to existing systems of power."[9] Put simply, a radical bookstore has the capacity to change the world. Because of this, bookstores are worth protecting.

## WHY DO BOOKSTORES *NEED* PROTECTING?

Despite the value they bring to their communities, bookstores are increasingly facing obstacles and even threats to their ability to do their work. One obstacle is the difficulty of making a career as a bookseller. Bookselling has a reputation as a demanding and low-paying job, for good reason. Retail work in general means a lot of contact with an often-unruly public, long hours on your feet, impossible customer demands, and physically grueling job duties. Benefits are few and far between, and they're often invisible. Rather than, say, PTO and health insurance, booksellers are often told that the perks of their job are advance copies of books and the opportunity to meet authors. The industry can get away with treating workers like this because bookselling is so often viewed as a calling. Of course I believe bookstores do important work, but it's also important to protect the people who do that work. Labor writer Kim Kelly writes, "It is an awful secret that so many of the workers who bring these cherished [books] to life are struggling with low wages, racial and gender inequities, and unsafe working conditions."[10] When I say bookstores must be protected, that means booksellers too.

Often, bookstore owners and managers point to the business's tight margins as a reason that higher compensation and benefits aren't possible. I see their point. Bookselling as it exists is an industry of scarcity. Corporate greed and consolidation are driving this crisis. You'd better believe top executives at behemoth publishers have wonderful pay and benefits, even as they offer cost-of-living raises that fall far behind inflation. Even as they bust up any unionizing efforts. These publishers tout record profits while bookstores can't make enough to properly pay their employees. At an even larger scale, Amazon, the country's biggest retailer of books, is in the middle of a decades-long campaign to make people think books are worth less than they actually are, which ultimately leads to less money flowing into the system. And less money flowing into the system means less money reaching those at the bottom (but again, of course, the people at the top are always going to be fine).

I don't want to protect bad bosses or unsustainable, underpaid bookselling jobs. I *do* want to protect the vibrancy of bookselling in general. Paying booksellers too little is not the answer. Answering scarcity with scarcity will do nothing except create a race to zero. The mindset that bookstores can scrimp and cut and whittle their way to a thriving bookstore industry is not sustainable. Trying to thrive by holding their breath will only find bookstores drowning in crises. We—readers, booksellers, publishers, community members—must find ways to make bookselling a sustainable career. Only then will bookstores find a bright future. That's why this book advocates for labor unions, higher minimum wages, alternative bookstore models, and other worker-friendly measures: the future of bookstores is booksellers, and they need to be protected.

While we're on the subject of booksellers, let's return to the claim that things are pretty good for bookstores right now: a surprising aspect of this current "indie bookstore renaissance," if you want to call it that, is that it's being driven by a historically diverse class of new booksellers and bookstore owners. In a July 2022 New York Times article, journalists Alexandra Alter and Elizabeth A. Harris claim that "the book selling business—traditionally overwhelmingly white—has . . . become much more diverse" because "many of the new stores that opened during the pandemic are run by nonwhite booksellers."[11] Stores from New York City (Yu and Me Books) to Los Angeles (the Salt Eaters Bookshop) and from St. Paul (Black Garnet Books) to St. Louis (the Noir Bookshop) have opened in the past few years under the leadership of new booksellers from historically marginalized backgrounds. In a January 2023 email, American Booksellers Association CEO Allison Hill told me that since January 2020, 96 new bookstores had been opened by self-identified people of color.

This diversification of booksellers is great news, especially considering the obstacles that kept bookselling so white in the first place. Opening a bookstore is staggeringly expensive—a new bookstore owner can spend hundreds of thousands of dollars in buildout, staffing, and initial inventory costs before a single book is sold. People of color, queer people, disabled people, and other marginalized groups have generally had a much harder time accessing that kind of capital. Therefore, most of the folks who have historically opened bookstores have come from backgrounds (read: white, upper and upper-middle class) that give them more access to capital and generational wealth. The fact that a new generation of booksellers is creative and persistent enough to work around this issue does not mean the issue is gone. And then there's this: opening a bookstore is a major challenge; but keeping it open is another. According to Gary Rivlin's book *Saving Main Street*, "One in three small businesses in the United States close before celebrating a second anniversary." Further, "Seventy percent are dead within a decade."[12] Because this exciting, diverse new generation of booksellers has overcome the once-insurmountable challenge of opening a store, and because they face a new set of major challenges in keeping their stores open, protecting bookstores is more important than ever.

Working in books is also growing more dangerous, especially for members of these marginalized groups. Somewhat unwittingly, bookstores and libraries (and the workers who make them tick) have ended up in the middle of a violent culture war. Reactionary right-wingers, including some at the very peak of influence within the national Republican Party, have seized on books as a battleground.[13] They primarily target children's books by queer authors and authors of color to force their regressive political vision onto America. The bookstores and libraries that disseminate these materials are therefore targets. Social media campaigns, verbal harassment, threatening phone calls, disruptive protests, and other social and political weapons are pointed at people who are doing the simple work of helping marginalized readers see themselves in books. Hundreds of Drag Story Hours have been disrupted by protestors spouting hate speech. A bookstore in Oklahoma faced harassment for making tee shirts with a QR code linking to a list of banned books. Personally, I received threats over Twitter for defending a fellow bookseller's right to free speech. As part of this online harassment campaign, people began ordering Mein Kampf from my store. As a bookseller, particularly a leftist Jewish bookseller, even writing this feels a little frightening to me. And for good reason: In November 2022, the Jewish-owned Iliad Bookshop in Los Angeles was the target of an arson attack, with rambling conspiracy-theory flyers left at the scene. Recently, Gretchen Treu, co-owner of A Room of One's Own Bookstore in Madison, Wisconsin, told me, "At one of our recent staff meetings, we were talking about what [happens] when someone comes in with a gun, because we're going to be a target. We're openly progressive, openly queer, openly trans, and that's getting scarier and scarier." Notice that Gretchen didn't say if someone comes in with a gun. Bookstores need to be protected.

# WHAT YOU'LL FIND IN THIS BOOK

There's much more to be said about the value of bookstores and the threats they face, and there's also another important question at stake here: How can bookstores be protected? This book aims to investigate all of this, in part through narrative profiles of 12 bookstores: Birchbark Books & Native Arts in Minneapolis, Minnesota; Avid Bookshop in Athens, Georgia; A Room of One's Own in Madison, Wisconsin; Shakespeare and Company in Paris, France; Red Emma's Bookstore Coffeehouse in Baltimore, Maryland; Bookends & Beginnings in Evanston, Illinois; Semicolon Bookstore & Gallery in Chicago, Illinois; Moon Palace Books in Minneapolis, Minnesota; Two Dollar Radio Headquarters in Columbus, Ohio; Biblioasis Bookshop in Windsor, Ontario; Loyalty Bookstores in Washington, DC; and Source Booksellers in Detroit, Michigan. Without exception, these are bookstores doing innovative and inspiring work in their communities. In different ways, they each demonstrate the amazing possibilities for bookstores in the 21st century. That's the primary reason I chose to write about them, but I also took into account a few other factors in creating the final list of bookstores to profile for this book.

First, geography. More than half of these stores are in the Midwest and Rust Belt of the United States; there are practical and philosophical reasons for this. In practical terms, it was important to me that this book be published by an independent publisher, especially one like Microcosm that refuses to do direct business with Amazon. Because of how the publishing industry works, going with a small independent publisher meant my advance for this book was $500, paid upon completion of the manuscript. That means I had to fund travel to each store on my own with my bookseller salary and royalties from my previous book, *How to Resist Amazon and Why*. Ultimately, for much of the process of researching this book, I had to focus on stores within driving distance of my home bases of Lawrence, Kansas, and Cleveland, Ohio. But this wasn't a limitation; I knew my beloved Midwest was home to terrific bookselling, and I also knew that the corporate media had a strong coastal bias. I'm not saying that there isn't amazing bookselling happening in New York and California; I am saying that midwestern stories get less national coverage than they should.

When deciding which stores to write about, I also took into account the historical forces that have maintained the barriers to entry in the bookselling world. In these pages you'll read about three Black-owned bookstores, one Indigenous-owned bookstore, one employee-owned co-op, and several bookstores that faced tremendous financial hurdles to open. One of my goals with this book is to outline these difficulties, yes, but also to show the amazing tenacity in people who find ways to do innovative bookselling work despite these obstacles. In addition to accounting for these economic and cultural considerations, I also aimed to create a list that represented a varied picture of what it means to be a good bookseller: from radical to traditional, from feminist to anarchist, from sleek to wabi-sabi, from a southern college town to the cultural capital of the Western world. The result, I hope, shows that an attempt to answer the book's central questions by profiling 12 good bookstores will lead to at least 12 answers.

At each bookstore I had an in-depth in-person conversation with at least one bookseller, often the store's owner (or one of them, if the store had multiple owners). I also spent significant time browsing and hanging out in each store, trying to experience it as a community member would. From the transcripts of the interviews and my impressions of each store, I built a narrative profile that attempts to engage with this book's central questions. Naturally, each profile speaks to different issues facing bookstores today. In the Avid Bookshop chapter, for instance, you'll read about the difficulties new booksellers face trying to attain traditional financing, while the Loyalty Bookstores chapter details the right's attacks on freedom of speech. My hope is that each profile forms part of a mosaic, and together they answer the questions of why bookstores are worth protecting, and why they need protecting.

After each profile, I've included action steps that zero in on specific answers to the question of how we can protect bookstores. These action steps are based on my zine *50 Ways to Protect Bookstores*; a lot of the content in these sections will be familiar to readers of the zine, but it has been updated for this book to reflect individual aspects of the 12 bookstores' stories. These steps are in part intended for individual consumers, yes, but I want to resist the idea that "voting with your wallet" is the sole answer to the question of how to protect bookstores. Shopping local is an important step, but it takes much more than that to create a world where bookstores and booksellers can thrive. That's why many of the book's practical suggestions are directed towards policymakers and others in power. Even if you're not a policymaker, you can certainly get in touch with the ones that represent you and tell them how much this issue means to you. The answers to the question "How can bookstores be protected?" are far-ranging and complex, but the same can be said for the issues and threats facing bookstores. Still, it is my core belief (and hopefully yours) that bookstores' contributions to their communities, as demonstrated by these 12 stores, make it all worth it.

# A NOTE ON POLITICS AND LANGUAGE

It's impossible to answer this book's questions in an apolitical fashion. The bookselling industry as a whole has become more political in the past few decades due to seismic external forces. According to Laura J. Miller's book *Reluctant Capitalists: Bookselling and the Culture of Consumption*, for a lot of the 20th century, "independent booksellers shunned controversy" in favor of "maintaining an image of conservative gentility."[14] But as the 20th century drew to a close, the mega-chains of Borders and Barnes & Noble became much more successful and powerful. This led to what Miller calls a "radicalization" of independent bookstores.[15] She explains: "By the end of the twentieth century, large numbers of booksellers were engaged in rhetoric and action they recognized as explicitly political . . . in ways that would have been hard to imagine just fifteen years earlier."[16] The most public manifestation of this newfound politicization of independent bookstores was a series of lawsuits by the American Booksellers Association targeting unfair wholesale discounting practices between the major publishers and Barnes & Noble. The days of headline-grabbing litigation by the ABA are over, but the politicization of bookstores lingers today.

One end result of this widespread politicization of bookselling is that many bookstores today have what you could call a voice, or a point of view. This point of view can be expressed in many ways: through a store's social media or newsletters, through the activism of individual booksellers, or through community political channels like city councils or trade associations. But it's important to note that the central act of bookselling itself—the stocking and shelving of books—is political. Often, a store's voice is expressed most clearly by what books are in the store and how they're arranged. The idea of politically minded curation was a central part of the feminist bookselling movement, where it was called "feminist shelfmaking." A few surviving feminist bookstores are carrying the tradition into the current day, as I'll explore in this book. But even outside of the feminist context, it is possible—perhaps more possible than for other types of retail—for a bookstore to carry a political point of view and, in doing so, become something more than simply a store.

It must be said that the orientation of this political bookselling work often leans left. That's certainly true, to varying degrees, of many of the bookstores profiled here. A few, like Shakespeare and Company and Red Emma's, have made explicit their leftist leanings. Others, like Moon Palace, have publicly shifted from left to more left. Still others are less overtly political but nonetheless would be considered liberal or progressive. The reasons for the politics expressed in this book are complicated; they reflect my own political orientation as an author and bookseller, as well as a general tendency in the industry. But I don't think the book industry is unfairly biased. If the industry leans left, one reason (at least lately) is that it's responding to the attacks from the right. As the right targets certain books, as well as those who read and write them, they are explicitly assaulting the very values that bookstores have long cherished: inclusion, community, literacy, and a diversity of voices. This book leans left, then, in part because—through book bans, violent demonstrations, and policies targeting things like drag shows and childhood literacy—the right wants to eradicate many things this book holds dear.

Of course, the further left someone goes on the political spectrum, the less likely they are to be comfortable functioning as part of the capitalist system. Herein lies an internal tension for many booksellers. As we've established, a bookstore is an effective mechanism for welcoming people into social justice movements. Many of those social movements are strongly opposed to the capitalist systems within which a bookstore operates, simply by virtue of being a for-profit business. As is true of all issues raised in this book, the booksellers I spoke to have different ways of approaching this. For some, it is indeed a moral dilemma to function in capitalism, causing political and emotional discomfort. Others are proud to sell things to their communities, classifying their work as commerce rather than capitalism. My goal is not to answer once and for all the problem of leftist booksellers functioning within capitalism, but simply to show you how 12 bookstores think about it at this point in their individual histories.

On another note, perhaps the seasoned reader of nonfiction about bookstores might have noticed that this book's title doesn't include the word "independent" or "indie." That is a conscious choice. Another consequence of the 1990s turn towards political bookselling was the coalescing of the idea of an "independent bookstore." Dan Cullen, former senior strategy officer for the American Booksellers Association, tells me he's pretty sure the term "independent bookstore" was invented to distinguish small, locally owned bookstores from national chains like Borders, Barnes & Noble, and B. Dalton. Indeed, according to Laura J. Miller, "an identity of independence, with its corresponding sense of solidarity and its expression of certain values, started to emerge after the establishment of the modern chain bookstores."[17] But are commonly held notions about the definition of "independent bookstore" expansive enough to cover everything a bookstore can do in 2023? I worry that when I say "indie bookstore," the reader will imagine one specific kind of place—maybe a tiny store. A store on a main street in a downtown row of storefronts. A quiet store. A store operated by a single owner. I even fear some people might make assumptions about what type of person becomes an "independent bookstore owner"—assumptions about age, race, class, and physical or mental ability. "Bookstore," being a broader term with fewer cultural assumptions associated with it, is useful in this project that seeks to broaden the idea of what bookstores can do. Additionally, given the demise of so many chain megastores and the rise of Amazon, I'm not sure the "indie" versus "not indie" distinction is quite so important anymore. Is a term invented to fight the big chains even that useful when the big chains are in dire straits? Of course, there are and always will be benefits to supporting locally owned small businesses instead of national chains, and I'll discuss those in detail in the pages to come. Still, the fight to protect bookstores has taken on a different tenor in the decades since "independent bookstore" came into use, and the language in this book reflects that.

## WHO IS THIS BOOK FOR?

Much of this book is about the inner workings of bookstores and the larger industry, so booksellers and other industry insiders are naturally part of its audience. But I don't want to write an inside-baseball book. Instead, I approach the topic in a way that I hope readers, community members, and fans of bookstores can also connect with. As with my previous project, *How to Resist Amazon and Why*, my goal here is to broaden the conversation. Just as the work of bookselling is about more than selling books, the challenges these bookstores face are bigger than bookstores; their causes, solutions, and consequences lie both inside and outside the industry. A better world for bookstores is also a better world for books, for readers, for communities. Thanks for being part of a conversation that tries to make that world possible.

# CHAPTER 1:
# "LAYERS OF COMMUNITY"
## Birchbark Books & Native Arts, Minneapolis, MN

*T*n many ways, the roots of this book were planted in March 2020. Broadly, the coronavirus pandemic reshaped the work of bookstores so significantly that it's impossible to write about contemporary bookselling without considering it. Narrowly, that's when I met Pulitzer Prize–winning novelist and bookstore owner Louise Erdrich, when she came to Lawrence for an event hosted by my bookstore, the Raven. That evening with Louise was my first exposure to the way she values bookstores and the inspiring way she fosters literary community. My learning about Louise's work happened right as the seriousness of the pandemic was setting in; her event was on March 11, 2020. Both events reshaped how I think about bookselling—an awakening that's still ongoing. Because of all that, she was the first person I interviewed for this book. So to start things off, I'd like to revisit an account of Louise's visit to Lawrence, which I first drafted in the chaotic weeks afterwards and revised for this book.

• • •

At 4:30 p.m. on March 10, I get a text from Chris. Chris is the inventory manager at the Raven, the bookstore where I work in Lawrence, Kansas. Chris texted, simply, "Louise Erdrich is here." That's not the kind of text you ignore.

Of course I knew Louise Erdrich would be in Lawrence, but I didn't know she'd be here a day early. I'm in the middle of a diaper change when I get the text. Then, in a whirl, I'm in the car, buckling the car seat, flying across the bridge in two minutes. Thank goodness there's a parking spot. I burst into the store and Louise is still there. We introduce ourselves, I introduce her to my son, she talks to him about the digger on his shirt. Later, my wife would ask my son about meeting Louise, and he'd point to his shirt and say, "digger," nodding. Louise says kind things about Lawrence. She says kind things about the store. If you've been spellbound by Louise's voice on one of her audiobooks, know that her voice is just like that in real life.

She says she'd love to grab dinner if anyone's interested.

At this point I'm trying not to be too effusive. I try to keep my cool around authors, something I've had to teach myself how to do. It's awkward to be fawned over. But Louise Erdrich is really, truly one of my favorite novelists. Not only that, she'd been in the number one spot on my author event wish list for years. The same was true for our partners on the event, Lawrence Public Library and Haskell Indian Nations University. Countless times I had answered "maybe someday" to someone asking when the Raven could bring Louise Erdrich to town. Now someday is tomorrow and Louise wants to get dinner tonight.

"Oh, okay, cool, I can send some texts." This is turning out to be a perfectly normal day. I duck into the other room to make a few calls. I call all the booksellers who requested to work the event. Kelly, Kami, and Nancy are free. I call Kristin, the events coordinator at Lawrence Public Library. She asks if she could bring Kathleen, director of development. Sure. I call Carrie, the librarian at Haskell, where the event will be held. Carrie says she can make it. A plan is hatched to meet in the lobby of the Eldridge Hotel at six and then head to 715, Lawrence's nicest restaurant. The plan works for Louise. It's 5:15. I head home to drop off the kid and catch my breath.

Dinner is an absolute joy, and that's not only because it's my last time sitting in a restaurant with a large, boisterous group until years later.

The next day's author event is set to take place at Haskell Indian Nations University, a campus in southern Lawrence with roughly 1,000 students from 140 federally recognized tribes. Twelve of its buildings, including the auditorium where Louise will speak, are National Historic Landmarks. Yet, to much of Lawrence's population, the smaller of Lawrence's two universities is a mystery, a blank spot. Except for during the immensely popular art fair in September, many Lawrencians never set foot on Haskell's campus.

In some ways, having Louise's event at Haskell made sense. It was Carrie the Haskell librarian's idea. Louise is a hero to many people, of course, but especially to the Indigenous writers and readers and teachers at Haskell. But it also posed a challenge—not many townies make it out there. The auditorium doesn't really have an address, per se. Three times I asked Carrie what the auditorium's capacity was, and I got five answers. There's not really any parking. This all seemed like it could hurt our numbers, and for an author like Louise Erdrich, numbers are how you convince the publishers to send more authors. But Carrie, with her contagious enthusiasm, convinced us. It made the whole thing more exciting, but more unpredictable at the same time. Even at 6 p.m. on March 10, a mere 24 hours before Louise's talk, I still had no idea what was going to happen. And that's before I even thought about the looming pandemic.

Before the Raven's author events I'm always afraid that nobody will show up (it's happened before). But today I'm also afraid that people *will* show up. What if nobody comes and we have to report bad numbers to HarperCollins for one of our highest-profile author events in years? *Or*, what if the auditorium, loaded with old and immunocompromised people, becomes a coronavirus hot spot? I had been scrutinizing state, local, and national guidance for large events. At that point, nobody suggested cancelling events under 500 people, and that's all we could physically fit in there. But still, could I trust the folks issuing guidelines? If it all goes south, I think, at least last night's dinner was fun. At least a few Haskell students got to meet Louise. At least she fell in love a bit with Lawrence.

Earlier that week, I'd actually scored eight 12-ounce bottles of hand sanitizer. The Raven's office supplies distributor still had some. Three came with us to Haskell, stationed at each front door. The library also brought their freestanding tower with the laser-activated touch-free dispenser. Kristin says she's seen people filling their own dispensers from it before the library closed. By now I've grown used to the feeling of hand sanitizer burning into cracked knuckle skin, but it was still new to me back then.

I go to the hotel to fetch Louise and we head south to Haskell. All day on Twitter I've watched people publicly announce their decisions to not attend tonight's event, their abundances of caution, their regrets. They stopped short of blaming us for doing something dangerous, but I still feel unsure.

Much later, I still won't be sure it was the best idea to carry on with it. But we do. In the end, 450 people show up. They give Louise a standing ovation before she says a single word. Maybe, like me, they feel like this could be the grand finale for anything we can safely call "normal."

Louise speaks beautifully. Many of the anecdotes she shared at last night's dinner—her family's history at Haskell, her daughter's pet crows—weave themselves into her stories, and the stories about the book, and beautiful passages she reads aloud. It's like a poetry reading. Nobody in the audience stirs. Nobody in the audience crinkles any wrappers. Nobody in the audience coughs, thank goodness. We sell so many books. We touch so many credit cards.

Finally, finally, the signing line dies down. The last of the books is inscribed. Louise and I say bye to Carrie and thank her with big hugs. We walk up the aisle and out of the auditorium into the crisp night of the Haskell quad. There is a small fire burning with a lone silhouette kneeling close. Louise says, "The students lit that sacred fire to bless this event. Let's go thank the fire's caretaker."

As we walk over to the fire, the caretaker stands, unfolding his lanky frame. He nods at us. Louise crouches and pulls some sage out of her bag. She crumbles off a few pieces and tosses them into the fire. They miss, landing on a cool spot away from the flame. She reaches her hand right in there and grabs the sage, placing it directly on top of the embers. She doesn't flinch.

Standing, she says, "Thank you for tending this fire. What's your name?"

"Junior," the caretaker says. "Yours?"

"I'm Louise, and this is Danny."

Junior reaches across the fire to shake our hands. It is my last handshake.

•   •   •

Our event at Haskell was Louise's last big author event, and the Raven's. It was the night Rudy Gobert tested positive for Covid and the NBA cancelled all its games. It was the night Tom Hanks announced he had caught it. It was the night that the whole thing began to feel very real, at least for me and the Raven's booksellers. It was the night Louise answered her daughters' pleas to come home: as she told me in the car on the way to Haskell, "I'm cancelling the rest of the tour. I'm headed home tomorrow. My daughter doesn't want me going to Chicago." When I wrote about the people in the crowd thinking the event was "the grand finale for anything we can safely call 'normal,'" I had no idea how right I was.

Looking back on March 2020, the main thing I remember is how the Raven had to adapt, and quickly. We shut down for browsing and tried a "pizza counter" model for a few weeks, and then went fully remote. In a period of weeks, we reinvented our business. That's true of all bookstores. The process of how bookstores did this is widely documented—I was even quoted in a *New York Times* article on the subject.[18] Article after article appeared, helping customers follow their bookstores into strange and difficult new territory.

A bit more than two years later, "normal" is still something that eludes the American bookstore, but that doesn't stop me from heading north to see one of the best. I stand in Louise's store, Birchbark Books & Native Arts in Minneapolis, soaking in some kind of magic. Louise's daughter Pallas is at the desk, apologizing for not wearing her Raven sweatshirt today. I ask her if she still has the crow friends and she does. Louise isn't here yet, so I take the chance to look around. Maybe it's just because I've read Louise's novel *The Sentence*, which features a ghost in a lightly fictionalized version of Birchbark, but there is some kind of special vibe in this place. I'm rarely a mystical person, so I can't describe it in too much detail, but the air is thick with *something*. A lot of people get wishy-washy describing bookstores, saying things about the smell of books or how the air is thick with stories. Generally, my view of bookstores is a bit more pragmatic. But not when I'm at Birchbark. Louise herself describes the feeling in her memoir, *Books and Islands in Ojibwe Country*, when she writes, "This little bookstore is where I belong and where anyone can belong. It is a home for people who love books and a place that cannot be duplicated by any bookstore corporation—it is just too personal."[19]

Tucked onto a quiet street across from a school in Minneapolis's Kenwood neighborhood, Birchbark's tiny confines are bursting with charm, character, and an unnamable *something else*. A canoe hangs from the ceiling. A confessional booth looms by the hallway to the back room. A sign in the confessional warns customers to stay out because Birchbark's insurance doesn't cover damnation. A maze of shelves fills the tiny room, bursting with new, notable, and hard-to-find books about and by Indigenous people. A newly installed section boasts a selection of language-learning books about Indigenous languages at risk of dying off. Birchbark simultaneously feels like the platonic ideal of a bookstore, and a bookstore so unique as to defy imagination. On their website, under "Our Story," Birchbark declares, "We are different from all other bookstores on earth!" And they're right.

Louise arrives. She gives me a big hug. We've spoken on and off, but we haven't seen each other since that day in March 2020. Before she can say anything beyond hello to me, the bell over the door chimes and an elderly customer clutches the railing and begins to labor up the steps. Louise cries out and rushes to help the customer into the store. Clinging to the Pulitzer Prize winner's arms, the customer asks about her special order. Only after answering the customer's question and making sure her feet are firmly planted on the creaky wood floors does Louise turn to me and start to chat. We make plans to take a walk around the neighborhood. But before we can do that, in the 10 short minutes we spend chatting in the store, Louise stops to handsell a book of Native folklore, straighten some shelves, and gracefully accept tearful compliments from one of her self-described biggest fans.

Since its founding in 2001, Birchbark Books has quietly blossomed into a neighborhood anchor and an important source of Native books, arts, and community. Carrie, the Haskell librarian, regularly sources hard-to-find books by and about Native people from Birchbark, happily driving up I-35 for a few hours to visit her friend Louise. While some of the customers I see are clearly there to spot the famous owner, many others are doing regular neighborhood bookstore things like browsing or chatting or placing orders. This is not a Louise Erdrich vanity project. This is a community-oriented bookstore doing important work. But this quietly impactful tiny bookstore in Minneapolis has humble beginnings: Louise's daughters wanted a cat, and her business plan was centered on an iguana.

When I ask her about her inspiration for opening the store, Louise has two answers. First, she says, "My sister Heid, who lives here, has been a mentor for Native students. My other sister and brother-in-law have been Indian Health Service doctors on reservations and their Indian health board. My brother is on the Indian Health Service. They all have something that they do for the Native community. This was mine." She pauses and thinks for a minute. Then she says, with a grin, "A lot of it had to do with not wanting a cat in the house. My daughters wanted a cat, and they thought we could have a cat if we started a bookstore. That was really important to them."

Perhaps this is one reason why Birchbark has such an impeccable, impossible-to-describe feeling. It's a family operation. That's a cliché at this point, but few stores embody it like Birchbark. Louise's daughter is at the register. Much of her family lives within walking distance. The entire idea was based on family, whether it be her sisters' service to their community, or her daughters' desires for a cat. In her memoir, Louise writes, "I started it with my daughters for idealistic reasons—the native community, the neighborhood, the chance to work on something worthy with my girls."[20] For a bookstore owned by a world-class author who's won the most prestigious awards possible, it feels really humble. In fact, it's so humble that to initially furnish it, Louise relied on the ancient art of trash-day scavenging: "There are easy chairs that I've plucked from neighborhood alley dumpsters or boulevards, where they've been left for the taking."[21] When you realize the whole thing started as an experiment in attaining a pet, it begins to make sense. Louise never did end up getting a cat. At some point in the process, the hypothetical bookstore cat turned into a hypothetical bookstore iguana. "This was my business plan," Louise says. "We'll make a confessional into the iguana thing." Fetching an iguana from a far-off reservation proved too big of a logistical challenge, but the bookstore and the confessional remained part of the plan and the bookstore was born.

From its humble iguana-focused business plan, Birchbark grew into one of the Midwest's most charming and wonderful bookstores. Even more importantly, it became a way that Louise could join her sisters in building and enriching the Indigenous community. That goal still guides her today. From the outset, Birchbark has been focused on Native art as well as Native books. Louise explains that on a reservation, "there's no outlet that is going to pay you enough for your work." She adds that "a big reason why I started the bookstore" was to provide a well-paying place to sell art by Native people year-round on a permanent basis. And lest you think capitalism isn't the way to uplift a community, Louise's vision of commerce is based more on humans than capital. She says,

> The marketplace has always been on many levels about community. Going to a huge supermarket is so much different from going to a farmer's market, because you're going to buy from the person who made it, right? You're going to buy from a small enterprise and you find out who's making your food, you find the human beings who are making the food that is sustaining you.

The same can be said for the Native art Louise sells at Birchbark. As much as this phrase can sound like a contradiction, it's a human transaction. Louise drives to reservations or even prisons to buy artwork directly from its makers, then drives back to the store to sell it. In so setting up the bookstore to highlight Native books and artwork, Erdrich has positioned her small experiment in a way to serve what she calls "layers of community." She explains:

There's Indigenous people. And then there are people who want to find out more about Indigenous people, so they come in knowing that there's going to be a lot to read. And there's also academic people who come in and say, "Well, I didn't even know this existed, or you can't get this book anywhere else." We also deal with very small presses, very unusual presses, Canadian presses, presses all over the world.

The layers of community go beyond even readers; a few yards away from the bookstore is the only nude beach in the Twin Cities. Louise tells me that "one of our other business models was to have the only working bathroom in the whole neighborhood," thus serving the nude bathers. Describing what happened in Birchbark's bathroom in the nude beach's heyday, Louise can only say, "God knows. It was pretty *wow*." Still, that's the community, and Birchbark found a way to serve it.

By this point in our leisurely chat, Louise and I have wandered across the street to sit on a bench under the biggest lilac bush I've ever seen, fragrant and exploding with blossoms. A passerby, surely recognizing Louise, offers to take our picture. Louise hands her her phone. We smile. After taking four or five shots, the photographer returns Louise's phone and walks off into the picturesque neighborhood, smiling. As we gaze at the low-slung building ("literally bricks and mortar," as Louise says) that's housed Birchbark from the beginning, we reflect on what might make this thing called bookselling any easier. Louise dearly misses when the other space in her building was a coffee shop and its walk-in traffic spread to Birchbark. She thinks bookstores and coffee shops are both "public commons, and that's something that Amazon can never be." Though Birchbark enjoys a high profile and a famous owner, plus a supportive neighborhood, Louise says the bookstore industry as a whole is "now contented with the crumbs of what it was." She adds that Birchbark has "enormous trouble just making payroll, and we want to be able to pay our people." I ask Louise what would make it better. The talk, of course, turns to Amazon. She says, "Amazon got what they wanted. They nearly killed it and they might still. They don't need books anymore. It's like a terrible marriage. Just let us go, just let us be, leave us alone." I ask her if things would instantly get better if Amazon stopped selling books. She says, "It would be really slow. We've been practically beaten into the earth."

Still, Louise remains optimistic and committed to the small work of building community through a bookstore. For one thing, she believes in the lasting power of the book itself. Louise says the book is like "the fork, the spoon, like things that you would dig up from the Dawn of Humanity. Books are one of those inventions, that's how I see it. There's nothing more perfected for human beings than a well-made trade paperback at this point." Additionally, Louise remains committed to the small and creative work of community bookselling. She says,

> We'll do whatever we can because that's how little bookstores have been. I mean, we're sponsoring a seed bank this spring. We contribute to different school prizes or enterprises. If we have a surplus of books, we bring them to the local library or to the local Indigenous coffee shop. We just try to do what we can to make ourselves more a presence. Whether it's events, whether it's donations, whether it's raising money for Standing Rock or for Line 3, we just start naturally. Whatever comes up, we're there for that.

Taken individually, these things aren't earth-shattering or even that unique (though I've never heard of a bookstore sponsoring a seed bank). Collectively, they're a big deal, especially in this neighborhood, this community. Amazon has disrupted and exploded the book industry. In a separate but not entirely unrelated story, Birchbark Books has done a lot of quiet, good work in one neighborhood of one American city, especially for its Indigenous people. Even if Louise wanted to move or move on, she feels deeply tied to her neighborhood and her bookstore. She says, "Now we're here, and I can't leave."

•　•　•

And now, reader, we find ourselves considering this book's title question for the first time: How do you protect bookstores? The first and perhaps most important thing you can do to protect Birchbark and places like it looks a lot like what you're doing now: reading. Birchbark (like all of the stores in this book) is sustained by devoted communities; those communities look as different as the stores they follow, but they all share one thing in common: they're all readers, and they're readers that frequently make individual purchasing decisions that help protect their bookstores.

## ACTION STEP: BE A READER

As Louise Erdrich told me, "There's nothing more perfected for human beings than a well-made trade paperback." If you take full advantage of that fact, you're already on your way to protecting bookstores. Make books a part of your life. You don't even need to buy them from bookstores. You can check them out of the library. You can raid the Little Free Library in your neighborhood. You can steal them from your family members while they're at work. You can even (gasp!) read the books you already own. The reasoning is simple: if America is a nation of readers, it will by extension be a nation of bookstores. It's not a huge leap for a lifelong reader to become a lifelong member of a bookstore's community.

I'm not going to soothsay about the doom-and-gloom End of Reading. I'm not going to weigh in on how much people watch TV or look at their phones. The death of the book has been predicted many times and will be predicted many times more. I'll just put it this way: reading begets reading. If you spend some time with a book today—even a few minutes!—you're already on the way to protecting bookstores.

One great way to help yourself become and stay a reader is to join a book club. Even if it's just an excuse to drink with friends. Even if you just meet online. Even if you just kvetch about the books. Even if Tyler's picks always kind of stink. Even if you talk about the book for 5 minutes and then spend the next 90 minutes gossiping about you-know-who. Even if it's only three members. A book club helps you turn your reading life into a community endeavor, and a community can sustain you as a reader. The more you're sustained as a reader, the more you'll read. The more you read, the more you'll protect bookstores.

Once your book club is cooking, there's another way it can protect bookstores: by teaming up with them. Once you've got some picks ironed out, let your local store know. They may order a bunch so you know they're there. They could set them aside under the name of your book club, or even give you a discount. Even at a discounted rate, those sales might still be worth it to them. A monthly guarantee of just 5 or 10 books sold to a local book club can make a huge difference.

## ACTION STEP: MAKE PURCHASING DECISIONS THAT PROTECT BOOKSTORES

The best, easiest, and most fun way to protect a bookstore is to make a habit of buying books there. While many bookstores have adapted to a more online world, I'd argue that there's still no match for the experience of browsing in a bookstore. A good bookstore is a complex organism designed to slow you down and connect you with books, and the best ones do that trick very well. Jeff Deutsch writes that "the good bookstore sells books, but its primary product, if you will, is the browsing experience."[22] A well-designed bookstore space is something magical, a space that works to force you to slow down. For Pete's sake, Birchbark Books has an empty confessional and a canoe hanging from the ceiling; name another retail space in America that can say that. A bookstore can create an elusive quiet, a surprising peace that even I, lifelong habitant of bookstores, still find myself chasing.

In regards to protecting bookstores, though, buying books in person just makes the most sense for the bookstore. In high-minded terms, it's what the stores are designed to do. In practical terms, it makes the most economic sense. In-person buying bypasses the expense of shipping materials and the extra employee time it takes to process an online order. For another thing, it's fun for us. We like it. The positive customer interactions are what keep us going even when working in retail gets difficult. Selling books to you in our building is what we're set up to do, and doing it a lot will protect our futures.

I'll pause here to note that I understand that buying new books isn't an economic possibility for everyone. This is especially true as the price of books goes up due to paper shortages, supply chain challenges, and, you guessed it, corporate greed. As an answer, I'll voice my support of used bookstores as well. A used bookstore brings many of the same benefits to a community as a store that sells new books, with the added bonus that the books are more affordable. Additionally, buying used books is one way to allay concerns about the environmental impact of printing new books. And of course, I don't want the only answer to be "spend money." With that in mind, this book discusses several ways to protect bookstores that don't involve spending money at all. While selling books is of course our bread and butter, and the people buying books are a necessary component of that, it's far from the only way to protect bookstores.

If buying books in person from a bookstore isn't feasible—say, your town doesn't have a bookstore, or circumstances don't allow you to regularly visit a store—buying a book online is the next best choice. Nearly all bookstores have an online-buying option, and many of them sell books directly through their website (this is what we do at the Raven, and this is what Birchbark does). Buying books online directly from a bookstore as opposed to, say, Bookshop.org (see below) gives the bookstore a bigger cut of the book's price. When you buy a book in store, the store gets 40–46% of the sticker price. When you buy online, the store gets the same cut, but subtract the cost of shipping materials and the extra labor it takes to process an online order. Processing an online order is a complicated task, and often what stores charge for shipping and handling doesn't cover it all. Still, if you can't make it to a store for whatever reason, and you're still able to purchase books, grab those books via a store's website.

Aside from buying direct on a store's website, there are other ways to buy books online that protect bookstores. Bookshop.org is a startup alternative to Amazon, founded to sell books online in a way that helps bookstores. They're a certified B Corp, and their beneficiary is bookstores, which means they're contractually bound to give bookstores monetary support. Here's how Bookshop.org works: A bookstore can start an online storefront on Bookshop, adding branding and curated reading lists. The bookstore then earns 30% of each sale through their online storefront. Non-storefront sales also give a smaller percentage to bookstores. Additionally, regardless of whether a bookstore has a Bookshop storefront, they can get profit-pool payouts from Bookshop. On the fulfilment end, rather than going through a physical bookstore and its booksellers, Bookshop sales are processed by the warehouses of massive book wholesaler Ingram.

Reactions to Bookshop in the bookstore world are mixed. Some worry that Bookshop is taking away from direct bookstore sales, and others are concerned about the lower-than-normal margins on

Bookshop sales. Still others worry about Ingram, a rapidly consolidating mega-corporation and the only major book wholesaler in the United States, gaining more power via direct-to-consumer sales. Others, however, celebrate Bookshop's ability to give people a start in the book industry without the massive investment needed for a brick-and-mortar storefront. A Bookshop storefront doesn't require a physical space; many bookstores that started during the Covid pandemic began with a Bookshop storefront they used to raise money for further evolutions of their shops. This has enabled a huge number of new Black- and POC-owned bookstores to get a foot in the door. The question of how much Bookshop.org protects bookstores is a complicated one, but I tend to take the view that a company that provides an easy alternative to Amazon and that has distributed $23 million to bookstores to date is a net good.

When you do buy books from bookstores, it doesn't have to be just one book. Plenty of organizations give away books in large quantities: political campaigns, corporations, libraries, schools, you name it. I'd argue that bookstores are not only *a* place to coordinate these bulk buys; they are the *best* place to do it. By placing a big bulk order through a bookstore, you're going to get personalized attention from a bookseller who's going to make sure everything goes smoothly. (Try to get personalized attention from Amazon about anything.) You may even be able to negotiate a discount from the bookstore, because bookstores get better pricing on business-to-business bulk sales. Despite its reputation for low prices, Amazon is slowly raising its prices on books, and it's hard to guarantee that it has enough stock in one place for any given bulk order. Bookstores can work directly with you and the publisher to ensure that everyone gets what they need. In exchange for a personal bulk-order concierge and a good price, the bookstore gets a nice sale to help them keep the lights on. Increasingly, bulk sales are an important part of bookstore profit and loss sheets, so sending your bulk orders through bookstores is a good way to protect them.

You also don't have to hold a book in your hand to buy it from a bookstore: bookstores love preorders too. Many authors and publishers have done a good job explaining the importance of preorders. Preorders can help a publisher gauge demand to ensure that there are enough copies of any given book in its first print run. Perhaps more importantly, a book's first-week sales total includes all the sales leading up to its release date in addition to the sales immediately after its release date. And a big fat first-week sales total gives the book a better chance of ending up on bestseller lists. Being on a bestseller list is a good indicator for staying on a bestseller list, and that first week is a book's best chance.

What folks have explained less effectively is that all preorders count as preorders. There's a lingering belief among authors and readers that the only preorders that "count" are on Amazon, and that's just not true. Bookstores report their sales to the same places Amazon does. Further, there are a few benefits to preordering from bookstores: often, an author's local bookstore will team up with the author to coordinate signed and dedicated copies of the book. Plus, bookstores are generally more conscientious about the condition of books, so if you're a first-edition collector you're better off ordering from a bookstore. When you preorder from bookstores, the bookstore gets the economic benefit of guaranteed sales, plus lots of helpful data about what books are going to hit it big.

Another way to protect bookstores is to buy books all year, and to shop early for the holidays. In 2021 at the Raven, the fourth quarter accounted for 45% of the year's sales. Nearly half of our business happened in the last few months of the year, and we're not an anomaly in that regard. Driving this fall/winter sales bonanza, of course, is the Christmas holiday. But compounding the blitz is publishers' tendency to pack all the biggest releases into the end of the year. All of the post-presidency books by the Obamas have had November releases, for instance. This means lots of good Christmas presents, sure, but it also means chaos for the bookstores trying to keep these books on the shelves. The complicated and fragile system used to make books is stretched thinner than ever. The global supply chain issues arising after the worst of the Covid pandemic have been well documented, and bookstores feel that pain like everyone else. Contributing to this issue is a nationwide paper and printing shortage. Just as paper is getting monstrously expensive, printing presses are shutting down. On top of all *that*, many of these high-profile fall books appear with very little notice and very large print runs, making it harder to print other books. This is all to say that if you're interested in helping your bookstore successfully capitalize on the vital fourth quarter, shopping early for Christmas is a great way to do it. For instance, starting your holiday shopping in October gives a bookstore more time to navigate supply chain chaos, ensuring that their shelves are fully stocked for the entirety of the fourth quarter.

Of course, if you can't manage to snag one of those hot fall titles, or if you're shopping for someone finicky who seemingly owns every possible book already, a gift certificate is a great way to go. From our end, gift certificates represent a literal investment in our future. Usually, gift cards are purchased in November and December and spent in trickles throughout the year. That leads to a big cash infusion for us during those crucial fourth-quarter months, allowing us to pay those big bills, give out employee bonuses, and hopefully eke out a little bit of profit. Gift certificates are one of the simplest ways to protect bookstores: paying for future books now.

Finally, books aren't the only things on offer at a bookstore, and there's a good reason for that. As much as I harp about the importance of buying books from locally owned bookstores, it's a bit of a painful irony that books aren't the most profitable things we sell. Yes, our bread and butter doesn't make us a ton of money. As previously stated, a bookstore keeps 40–46% of the price of a book. If a book were to cost $5, that means a bookstore would keep around $2.30. Compared to other retail goods, this is actually a low markup. A movie theater, for instance, can keep up to $4.63 from the sale of a $5 bag of popcorn.[23] The reasons for the low markups on books are numerous and complicated, but they shake down to the perceived value of books, combined with the fact that nearly all books come with the price printed on them. This low-markup issue in books is one of the factors that leads bookstores to sell other things, like stationery, greeting cards, and notebooks, or the wonderful collections of Native art at Birchbark. These not only have better wholesale pricing than books; they also don't come pre-printed with the price. All this means that bookstores generally make a bit more money on non-book stuff than they do on books themselves. Additionally, many bookstores offer merchandise featuring their name and branding. So when you buy and wear bookstore merch, you're not only contributing to the store's profit margins—you're also helping it build recognition. And as an added bonus, wearing a bookstore shirt in public may even help you meet a fellow fan of the store.

The question of how to protect bookstores can get complicated, as you'll see in the following pages. That's because many of the challenges facing bookstores are systemic problems, tied up with a lot of other issues and concerns in politics, economics, and society. But the first step to protecting bookstores always starts at home, on the personal and local scale. Every thriving bookstore is built upon a supportive community of avid readers who make purchasing decisions that allow that bookstore to keep doing what it's doing. At Birchbark, that community includes everyone from nude swimmers to the local Indigenous community looking for hard-to-find language textbooks. Your bookstore's community will look different. The magic of it all is that your bookstore, if it's a good one, is working to meet your community's specific needs. At its best, this relationship is reciprocal. I don't think one person's decision about where to buy one book will make a huge difference to, say, Amazon, but it will make a huge difference to one small bookstore.

# CHAPTER 2:
# "WE JUST FIGURE OUT HOW
# TO MAKE IT WORK"
## Avid Bookshop, Athens, GA

*T*t's an unseasonably warm day in Athens, Georgia. This hilly southern college town feels cheerful today. Having spent so much time in Lawrence, Kansas, I have a proclivity for midsize college towns like this. But there's also something about the first warm day of the year that makes people, somehow, emerge. They wear shorts for the first time. They walk instead of taking the bus. They chat, they wander, they roam. Perhaps a part of the town-wide bonhomie today is the fact that the University of Georgia football team won the NCAA championship last night. But today is not a day of revelry. It's just a cheerful day in a lovely southern town. That seems like enough.

Amidst this pleasant milieu I'm sitting at a patio table outside of Avid Bookshop, just southeast of campus on Lumpkin Street. It's one of four small businesses on the sidewalk level of a historic brick apartment building nestled right up to this busy street. I'm slowly indulging in a rich sipping chocolate from Condor Chocolates, Avid's next-door neighbor. Across from me is Janet Geddis, owner and founder of Avid. Though there is a tape recorder between us, it feels like a casual conversation between old friends catching up. I've met Janet before. At one conference afterparty years ago, I fell in with the Avid crew for an amiable night of drinks and lukewarm appetizers. Still, it's been years since we've seen each other. Maybe it's this magic Athens air that makes the words come so easily.

It's my first time in Athens, and I'm only here for the night; even though my conversations with Janet and her team are wide ranging and frank, I won't purport to know about this town beyond the fact that I'd like to return someday soon. Like Lawrence, Athens is a progressive town in a state with a complicated political story. It has a reputation for being cool, for launching the B-52s and REM and the Elephant 6 collective. Everything I eat during my 24 hours in Athens is delicious. Also: during our interview, my back is to Avid's front door. Janet, across from me, is facing her store. Halfway through our conversation, Janet interrupts herself to tell me, under her breath, that Michael Stipe is walking into Avid. She waves.

From what I hear on my visit, this is a community-minded bookstore that's made some difficult choices about how to best serve its booksellers and customers. But it hasn't been sunny days and rock stars the whole way. For a long time, Janet wasn't even sure Avid would happen.

•   •   •

Janet came to bookselling, like so many others, in a roundabout way. Her story is perfectly indicative of how difficult it is for even the most enthusiastic, passionate, and creative people to successfully open a new bookstore. She left graduate school with a master's degree in educational psychology, hoping to work with the gifted students of Georgia's governor schools program, but, she tells me, "due to various political things, by the time I graduated, that was no longer an option." So, in 2007 or so, she joined the ranks of countless millennial under-employed, over-degreed humanities graduates. She started collecting gigs: "I was just nannying and tutoring and doing a bunch of things that I was good at, but I didn't ever look forward to it. Once I was there, I was fine, but I wasn't like, *Oh my God, I cannot wait to tutor today.*" In the middle of all this, Janet was exchanging letters with an old friend who was doing a semester teaching in a kind of roving classroom that stopped in a different place every night. "I would write her a letter to whatever post office box was at the next stop," she tells me, "so I wrote her a letter and was like, 'Hey, we always talk about opening a bookstore as a pipe dream, but what if we really looked into it? That would be cool.'" Then something wild happened. Janet tells me, "The next day I get my mail and there's a letter from her, and in essence, she's like, 'We always talk about this bookstore thing and I feel like we should maybe do it.'" Janet immediately called her friend and asked how she got access to such fast postal service, thoroughly confusing her friend. Turns out, her friend hadn't even gotten Janet's letter about starting a bookstore. Rather, she had simultaneously sent her own, unrelated letter. They both arrived at the same idea at the same time, hundreds of miles apart.

I'll interject here to say, from where I sit, Athens is a perfect place for a bookstore. It's an artistic and funky college town. It's pedestrian friendly. There are small businesses everywhere. There's a good library system. Because of the university, it has a highly educated population with lots of young families. As someone who's run a bookstore in a town just like that, let me tell you: these are ideal conditions for a bookstore. And Athens didn't have a bookstore like Avid yet. There was a dusty old used shop downtown, and a Barnes & Noble on the highway out of town, but there was no cozy shop selling new books with clever booksellers and author events and all that good stuff. Janet tells me, "I wanted a place where people's relationship with books was non-judgmental and really open and just encouraging exploration and joy around books, whether or not they bought something that day. It was really important to me that people felt welcome there." Janet's idea was a good one, and anybody who knows anything about bookstores and how they operate would've agreed. So in 2008, Janet and her friend announced they'd be bringing a bookstore to Athens.

If only it were that simple. For one thing, Janet's friend left the project the next year out of fears of what business debt would do to compound her already significant law school debt. This was frightening for Janet. As I can attest from experience, humanities graduate degree programs really don't prepare you to be a business owner, so going it alone can be intimidating. For another thing, Janet has long experienced chronic migraine, meaning some days she can't work at all. Her longtime friend understood this, and they had figured out ways to work together. Still, Janet decided to do it. And then things got really hard. It was 2008. She tells me, "I announced [my plans] right before the economy crashed."

Avid did open—in 2011, four years after the initial exchange of letters that kickstarted the idea. It wasn't just the economy; it was also the steep challenges faced by young entrepreneurs, especially women and folks from marginalized backgrounds, when it comes to securing capital to start a business. In many ways, Janet was a great candidate for something like this. She was doing her research about the book industry, winning scholarships to attend conferences and volunteering at other Atlanta-area stores. Further, as she tells me, "I had no debt at the time, blissfully." Still, she didn't have a ton of income. Because of this, and even with all her experience and preparation, Janet tells me, "It was really hard to get loans." One of her efforts to try to jumpstart Avid into existence was to join an Athens buy-local board, listing her business as "Avid Bookshop Coming Soon." Others on the board thought Janet's idea was surefire— she tells me, "On that board was somebody who worked at our local bank. And so I tried to work with her, and I worked with a small-business development center. And all these people were like, 'You're going to get this loan.' And then I would get rejected and they were like, 'This is crazy. I can't believe you got rejected from this.'" Janet tells me that the stated reason for the loan rejections was "often like, 'You've never had a loan in this amount before.'" As she points out, "It was ridiculous." A program specifically designed for first-time business owners rejecting applicants because they hadn't gotten a significant loan before—it certainly seems to me like that's eliminating the loan program's target audience right out of the gate. But I have heard story after story of people running into similar obstacles when trying to open bookstores, including the two founders of the bookstore where I work.

In the face of the challenges attaining financing, Janet shrunk her budget by 83%, from $300,000 to $50,000, thinking if she could just get open on a shoestring she could grow from there. But the obstacles kept coming: a friend offered to loan her the $50,000 but backed away when Janet wanted to commit the agreement to paper. So Janet kept searching. She applied for a small-business grant from Pepsi that meant they'd use the store to film ad videos. She asked Avid's Twitter followers if it was possible to use Kickstarter, then a young technology, to start a business. Indiegogo saw the tweet and offered to team with Avid, again exchanging support for the right to use the future store as a backdrop for commercials.

Eventually, Janet tells me, the banker on the buy-local board invited her to coffee. The banker had been thinking about Janet's plight, and the failure of the small-business startup grants to do what they're supposed to do. The banker had dreamed up a scheme. As Janet explains it, "My parents owned the house that I was living in. And so [the banker] was like, 'If they sign off on it, we could get a home equity line of credit. After a year, transition that into a business line of credit." Janet was determined not to ask her parents for money, but here was a way they could help that didn't involve writing a check. That, plus the modest sum raised from Indiegogo, plus a county-sponsored gap financing program finally allowed Janet to move forward with a brick-and-mortar location.

Even with funding finally in hand, opening a bookstore on a shoestring proved challenging. Renovating a building, purchasing initial inventory, and furnishing the space with fixtures can quickly eat into whatever funding has been patched together. For shelving, Janet purchased old fixtures from a closed Washington, DC, store called Chapters. (This is a common strategy—many bookstores have little bits of dead bookstores within them via the purchase of used fixtures. It's a fun game to ask a bookseller which defunct stores live on through their shelves. The Raven has shelves from the Wichita Borders and the much-missed Bluebird Books of Hutchinson, Kansas.) For labor, Janet stumbled upon a concept in the buy-local movement called the Time Bank. The idea is simple but radical: people volunteer whatever kind of services they specialize in. When folks take them up on their offers, the people providing the services earn Time Dollars to spend on other services. In the early days of Avid, people earned Time Dollars by clearing out the building, removing ivy from the walls, cleaning and painting the recycled shelves, and doing all kinds of other manual labor that Janet likely wouldn't have been able to afford otherwise. Even better than using this community strategy to ready her store, it gave people a deep sense of connection to Avid before it even opened. Janet tells me that the Time Bank labor "led to people coming in for years being like, 'I painted that wall. See that right there? I patched that floor.' Just this sense of ownership."

Ultimately, Janet and her team had a long and difficult four years between having a very good idea and that idea becoming a reality. False starts, difficulty raising money, and speed bumps abounded. An idea this good—a friendly, welcoming small bookstore in a lively college town—shouldn't be this hard to execute, especially in a place like Athens, especially with a person like Janet at the helm. Even more frustratingly, I'm not sure what useful lesson other prospective bookstore owners can learn from Janet's story. The steps that eventually led to success—the home equity line of credit, Indiegogo, the Time Bank—are all specific to Janet's situation. There should be a more detailed roadmap for young people to open a bookstore than just saying "it's going to be really hard and take a long time."

• • •

Eventually, once Avid opened, they found success. Their tiny storefront on Prince Avenue, a short drive from the location where I sit today, helped them become a central part of Athens's literary life. They hosted events, partnered with schools and local organizations, and did all the things the best bookstores excel at. Things were going so well, in fact, that Janet began thinking about adding another location.

In the process of opening the first Avid location, as she networked and met people and tried to gather support for her project, Janet kept hearing people tell her, "You've gotta meet Rachel Watkins." Janet didn't know Rachel, but everyone told her she was one of the bookiest people in Athens. So Rachel and Janet set up a "blind friend date" at Jittery Joe's, which is directly across the street from the current location of Avid on Lumpkin. It was a good match. Rachel says books "have always been my through-line." She was a former teacher, and a volunteer for a nonprofit called Books for Keeps. Needless to say, Rachel and Janet hit it off. During that first friend date, Janet looked across the street at this historic commercial row and said to Rachel, "Can I tell you a secret? That's the spot I want for Avid's second location."

Rachel responded, "You should rent it, then."

Janet said, "But it's not for rent."

Rachel said, "Didn't you see the email?"

Turns out, the owners of the spa that currently occupied the space were leaving and wanted to rent the space, and fast. To Janet, this seemed like an opportunity. Janet had always wanted to expand the original Avid space into the adjacent storefront, adding more square footage to allow for things like a back office and space to process school orders. But Janet had checked with the current occupants of the adjacent space on Prince, and they weren't intending to leave anytime soon. Still, sales kept increasing at Avid's original spot, which Janet took to mean that there was a need in the market for higher-capacity bookselling. If she wasn't going to fill it, someone else would. So in November 2016, five years after the first Avid opened on Prince, the second location cut its ribbon on Lumpkin.

For a while, the store functioned as a two-location operation. Then, after a year or so, Janet says sales started tapering, but not to an alarming degree. "Just enough that I was keeping an eye on it," she says. On top of that, Janet's personal life grew a bit turbulent; combined with the two-store model and the ballooning staff of more than 20 booksellers, Janet "felt like the connection I had to this store was kind of gone." This difficult situation led Janet to consider one of the hardest questions a business owner can ask: What is the right size of my business?

The American capitalist system is based on an idea of constant growth. It's a widely held notion that one good way to increase sales is to expand into more locations. The franchiser is viewed as a sterling model of American entrepreneurship. There's far less precedent for celebrating businesses that shrink, but I'd argue that finding the right size for your business is a much more sustainable goal than growth at all costs. Janet agrees. She tells me,

> So much is based on the capitalistic aspect of growth, growth, growth, growth. I don't think people even have models for small business to say, "We just want to keep

the doors open and feel kind of secure." I used to do a lot of talks and go meet with the UGA business school. I always made a point to say, "If you're interested in doing something that's just for you or your family or your town and you don't have your sights set on expanding or getting angel investors and stuff, yeah, that is just as legitimate as anything else. Come and talk to me if you want." And so many students have come up to me afterward being like, "Oh my God, I just really want to open a hair salon, and all of the classes in school are about IPOs."

It's okay to run a business with a goal other than growth and the generation of ever-increasing profit. A business owner can have community goals at the heart of their business plan. Or literary goals. Or a simple wish to provide a few good jobs for as long as possible.

I don't want to project thoughts into Janet's head, but one of the things that inspires me about Avid's story is Janet's willingness to step back and really ask herself if a two-store model was the best idea for her and the best fit for her business and its booksellers. She tells me, "In 2018, I started thinking about closing the Prince Avenue store. And then in 2019 I got more serious about it, but didn't bring it up to anybody. I just started doing numbers by myself, looking to see what would happen." In the midst of all this thinking, Janet started meeting regularly with Rachel and Luis, Avid's managers. She agonized over whether to share her thoughts on the Prince Avenue store. As she pondered this during one meeting, Luis simply brought it up for her, unaware of the year of thinking Janet had already done: "What if we close the Prince Avenue store?"

This was at the end of 2019. Not only does this story show a management team willing to ask difficult questions about the right size of their business; it also shows an amazing bit of foresight about what 2020 would bring for retail small businesses. But Rachel, Luis, and Janet didn't know that Covid was coming—they just knew that their current model had robbed some of the magic from what they did. Complicating things, their landlord wasn't budging on lease renegotiations for the Prince Avenue spot. Their inability to reach an agreement with the landlord ultimately pushed them over the edge, and the original Avid location closed on December 31, 2019. Reflecting on that time, Janet says, "Downsizing was difficult, but I genuinely feel like we did it from a position of relative strength. I wasn't freaked out. I was concerned with sales patterns and making sure we could meet payroll if numbers went down, but also I really was looking forward to revamping in 2020 and just having the small store." Though 2020 would bring challenges nobody was expecting, and though it was difficult to close the original Avid location, it wasn't without some measure of joy: on the last day before they handed the keys over, Luis and his husband got married with a group of friends and supporters in the empty store.

●   ●   ●

In later years, Janet and her management team have made a concerted effort to make sure Avid is a good place to work, a real challenge in an industry that has failed to let its successes trickle down to the part-time workers at the bottom of the ladder. Still, Avid has done what they can. They count a full-time work week as 35 hours, for one thing. For another, they have a generous paid family leave policy. When I ask Rachel how they can afford paid family leave when so many other bookstores would say they couldn't, she simply says, "We just figure out how to make it work." Really, it's a question of what Avid prioritizes; as Rachel says, "We put so much into our staff that retaining them is so important. And to me, that means family leave and paid time off and having a voice at staff meetings." During the Covid shutdown, Avid started weekly check-in meetings with staff, which combined emotional support with practical business matters. Rachel tells me, "The most logical thing to do at those meetings was to do a check-in on how you're doing personally. Especially during Covid, to have a space to be like, 'I'm really scared I can't read' (which is what our job is), that really was helpful." Additionally, starting in 2020, the leadership team of Rachel, Luis, and Janet spent eight months meeting weekly with Krystle Cobran, Athens's first inclusionary officer. This better prepared them to handle microaggressions, prejudice, and outright racism when it came up. And this being retail in the 21st century, it always comes up.

In the spring of 2018, Avid was gearing up for a two-day book fair with a private school in Athens that they'd worked with before. As usual, the school requested some titles to include in the fair, and they also welcomed the inclusion of, for instance, books that had been nominated for the Georgia Children's Book Awards. Janet tells me, "I don't know that we ever gave [the school] a complete final list to approve because the understanding was you bring what you want, I trust you as long as it's in these parameters, including the Children's Book Award nominees, or whatever."

During the book fair, Janet got a text from Caleb, one of the Avid booksellers staffing the event, who just so happens to be a gay man. A dad browsing the book fair had seen a copy of Richard Peck's *The Best Man*, a middle-grade book with gay themes. The book was a nominee for the Georgia Children's Book Award that year. The father picked it up and handed it to Caleb, requesting it be removed. As Janet tried to figure out what to do, the father escalated things by complaining about the book's presence to the principal. Historically, the principal had been supportive of Avid's involvement, pushing for them to do the school's book fair instead of Scholastic. Janet talked to her staff, paying special attention to queer staff members, and they decided the only way they'd continue with the book fair was if the school issued a statement apologizing and reinstated the book on the table. The principal, facing tremendous pressure from a growing group of parents, not only said "I can't do it" but also requested a full school-led review of all Avid's selections for "objectionable content." So Janet and a few other staffers went to the school the next morning and retrieved all the books. Then, they decided to do an in-store book fair with the remaining stock. They donated 10% of that day's sales to the Athens LGBTQ Youth Group. Avid wrote a post on Facebook explaining their stance, saying, in part,

> Complaints from parents unwilling to admit to their children that gay couples exist turned into a call to remove an entire section of our community from the book fair within minutes. We were told this was the "path of least resistance," but we believe it is our duty to ensure that the path of least resistance is not always at the expense of the marginalized. . . . Much of our staff identifies as queer or LGBTQIA+, and Avid Bookshop's mission has always been one of inclusivity, kindness, and understanding.

Here is a business making a decision that's bad for business—scrapping an entire planned second day of a book fair—to stand up for its principles and protect its queer employees. It's a pretty powerful gesture, one that caught the attention of *The Best Man* author Richard Peck himself. In a *Publishers Weekly* column about the incident, Peck writes, "Is there hope ahead here? Maybe, cautiously." Unfortunately, the culture war surrounding queer books has only intensified in the years since 2018. Still, it's heartening to know that there are bookshops like Avid that will ask difficult questions about how best to support their employees, choosing that route over the bottom line every time.

•　　•　　•

A key part of Avid Bookshop's story is how hard it was for Janet to go from idea to bookstore. It took four years of hard work and trying every possible idea, often leading to dead ends and discouragement. Through it all, Janet doggedly created a voice for Avid on social media, even though there was no brick-and-mortar Avid quite yet. When she opened her doors, she had already done some work building her community, and they were ready to go, not only as shoppers, but as volunteers to help finish Avid's space. Janet's use of social media to form her store's personality and philosophy before it even had a location is indicative of how much of the bookstore experience can actually exist online. The fact is, there are a lot of free, online-only ways to protect bookstores.

## ACTION STEP: INTERACT WITH BOOKSTORES ONLINE

Alas, this may be getting more complicated in a rapidly shifting social media landscape. While I was working on this book in late 2022, Twitter was embroiled in a rushed takeover by Elon Musk, who seemed more interested in his own ego than in running a functional social media network. In another corner of the internet, Facebook and its subsidiary Instagram seem more interested in building a bad virtual reality world than any kind of good user experience. In November 2022, Facebook announced 11,000 layoffs. Around the same time, TikTok announced a plan to sell books directly to customers in the app, cutting out many of the bookstores who create content to make BookTok tick. (Of course, that'll only work if the US government doesn't ban TikTok first, something that's looking increasingly likely.) I'm not sure what the future holds for social media, and for bookstores on social media in particular. I say this with sadness as a bookstore owner (and, honestly, an author) who's achieved a bit of success thanks to social media.

But although the future is uncertain, in the present, at least for now, social media remains one of the ways bookstores can connect with their communities online. On top of that, the flawed measure of follower count still holds some weight—for instance, if two stores are in contention to land a big author event, the publisher may use social media follower counts as a kind of tiebreaker. So before the whole thing teeters off into the digital void to make room for whatever's next, a free and effective way to protect bookstores (and ensure they can communicate with their communities) is to follow a bunch of them on social media.

Of course, a successful social media presence requires that your content be seen—not buried under promoted posts. This is getting harder to pull off. One way to help bookstores defeat the algorithm is for folks to talk to bookstores or tag them in their posts. After all, that's how Avid started building its community long before it managed to open a physical storefront—talking to people online. It still helps for bookstores that are long established. Buying a book from a bookstore? Make an Instagram post about it and tag us (tag the author too, as long as you're saying nice things!). Feeling good in your bookstore merch? Tag us in the photo! This might help us avoid getting lost in the algorithm, and even if it doesn't, it'll bring a smile to our faces.

So if social media is growing less reliable or useful for bookstores trying to communicate with their communities, what's going to replace it? I can't speak for everyone, but I'll tell you the Raven is doubling down on our email newsletters. The newsletter format is much easier to cram with information. Even better, we can control who sees what without rolling the algorithmic dice. Lots of bookstores put really good stuff in their newsletters—staff reviews of forthcoming books, glimpses into the day-to-day operations of the business, event information, and more. From where I sit, the bookstore email newsletter is the best way to get information from a store, short of actually going in and asking someone a question. By subscribing to and reading a bookstore's newsletter, you are joining its community and therefore helping to protect it.

## ACTION STEP: MAKE IT EASIER FOR PEOPLE TO START SMALL BUSINESSES

Of course, Janet's clever social media work was born out of necessity. Given the choice, I'm sure she'd elect to not be forced to work as a Twitter-only no-books-actually-sold bookstore for four years. At least in theory, there are programs out there that should allow an entrepreneur with a good idea and a lot of research under their belt to open a small business, regardless of how much money they have on hand. But Janet's story, and many others, show that these programs remain out of reach to even the most promising and talented aspiring small-business owners. An example of this hits very close to home for me. In 1986 and 1987, when college friends Pat Kehde and Mary Lou Wright decided they wanted to open a bookstore in Lawrence, Kansas, they talked to several banks. None of the banks offered them business loans. A few dismissed their idea as a hobby, not a business. Eventually, Pat and Mary Lou collected some small loans from friends, and one of them refinanced their mortgage much like Janet did with the house her parents owned. So, despite the lack of financing, their business persists to this day as my bookstore home, the Raven.

You know what else persists? The difficulty in obtaining startup funds for small businesses, especially for women and people of color. Without access to generational wealth, the amount of money needed to successfully start and stock a bookstore is easily out of reach. Bank loans and support from the Small Business Administration require jumping through hoops and writing complex business plans. Gathering these materials can be a tremendous strain on someone who also has to work a full-time job to support themselves. Plus, applicants are easily denied even if all that stuff is ready to go. This functions as a barrier to entry, allowing only those who already have money to easily start up bookstores. There's no easy answer to this systemic issue, though policy suggestions in later chapters might offer a starting point. Community-oriented solutions, including micro-loans and crowdfunding, also help—Avid was one of the first bookstores to use an online crowdfunding platform to raise capital, and many more have followed suit. Really, any action that makes it easier for potential booksellers to acquire capital and start their businesses would be a critical step towards protecting bookstores.

## ACTION STEP: PATRONIZE AND PROTECT YOUR LIBRARY

Another key aspect of the Avid story is that Athens is a great place for a bookstore, which makes it that much harder to believe it took four years for Janet to find funding to open one. One of the things that makes Athens a good spot for bookselling is a strong public library system. Not only that—the libraries work closely with Avid, creating a symbiotic relationship that's common to many great bookstores and libraries. Indeed, when I asked Avid's Rachel Watkins to describe her relationship with Athens libraries, she called it "fabulous." Like Avid and their libraries, the Raven and the Lawrence Public Library are best buds. We host events in their auditorium all the time. We sponsor their events and donate stuff to their fundraisers. They advertise on our walls. We sell books when they bring in big authors. In countless ways, LPL and the Raven work together to bolster literary life in our community. I don't think this arrangement is unique to Lawrence, Kansas, either. Libraries and bookstores have a lot of differences, but I maintain that they share at least one core goal: to build a community of engaged readers. We already know that a good way to protect bookstores is to place them within such a community. Libraries help with that work. Alarmingly, though, libraries are increasingly under attack as part of a vicious, right-wing-led culture war.

To highlight just one example of the nationwide wave of attacks on libraries, I can again look close to home: just down the road from the Raven in St. Marys, Kansas. The story of the St. Marys library shares a lot with the story of Avid and the book fair: in both stories, right-wingers wanted to attack queer books as a way to limit the books an entire community had access to. In late 2022 the St. Marys branch of the Pottawatomie Wabaunsee Regional Library in Kansas was up for a lease renewal on its building. Normally a routine local-government operation, this time around the library's lease renewal turned into a front in the culture wars. A parent in St. Marys was upset to find his child interested in Alex Gino's *Melissa*, a YA book with a transgen-der protagonist. The father insisted that, since it had a transgender character, nobody should be able to get this book from the St. Marys library. But before he could even submit a formal challenge to the library, the St. Marys City Council proposed a morality clause to be included in the library's lease. The clause stipulated that "the library not 'supply, distribute, loan, encourage, or coerce acceptance of or approval of explicit sexual or racially or socially divisive material, or events (such as "drag queen story hours") that support the LGBTQ+ or critical theory ideology or practice.'"[24] The St. Marys library re-fused to sign the lease containing the clause, causing the city coun-cil to consider "creating their own city library, one without 'divisive material.'"[25] (When Avid was challenged in a similar fashion, the principal went after "objectionable" content, and here the St. Marys City Council is looking for "divisive"—be wary of anyone using these words as stand-ins for, for instance, "queer" or "Black"). The situa-tion came to a head in a series of city commission meetings in early winter 2022. Each time the commission met to discuss the issue, li-brary supporters flooded the chambers in solidarity with the library and the tireless work of library director Judith Cremer.

Ultimately, the commission renewed the library's lease without re-strictions, despite the months of threats. What made the difference?

According to *Kansas Reflector* reporter Rachel Mipro, "Commissioners said the outpouring of public support for the library informed their decision to extend the lease by one year."[26] This is how you save a library and defend free speech, and it's a playbook that can be used when bookstores face the same kinds of attacks: Show up. Make noise.

# CHAPTER 3:
# "OPENING THE DOORS MORE"

## A Room of One's Own, Madison, WI

*W*hen Gretchen Treu moved to Madison, Wisconsin, for college in 2003, they were, in their words, "a little baby gay." After arriving in town to commence their studies at the University of Wisconsin, Gretchen cast about for places that felt comfortable in their new city. This led to them "awkwardly" hanging around at the local feminist bookstore, A Room of One's Own. Room, as it's often known, was founded in 1975 as part of a movement of feminist bookstores across the country. There were more than 100 of them; they shared a mission of supporting feminist causes and disseminating feminist texts. They shared a commitment to stocking books by and about women, almost exclusively. They shared tactics and ideas and a widely circulated newsletter. They influenced a lot of people, including Gretchen.

Indeed, it was within Room that Gretchen found a welcoming place as a "baby gay." Like in so many of these stories (including my own), hanging around the bookstore turned into working at the bookstore. At the time, Room had a co-op coffee shop, and in 2005, some of the workers there approached Gretchen about helping out part-time. When the coffee folks asked Gretchen for help, Gretchen's response was "Wow! Me? Little me?" The coffee slingers responded, "Yeah. Literally, please help us." Eventually, fate drew Gretchen from behind the coffee counter and into the shop. A self-described "book person," Gretchen had worked at libraries and volunteered at bookshops throughout their high school years. In 2007, upon returning to the Room coffee counter after a semester abroad, Gretchen found that one of the part-time booksellers was leaving. Store brass told Gretchen to apply, since their getting the job was basically a sure thing. They applied, and got the job, and immediately took to bookselling. So much of Gretchen's story is about being in the right place at the right time. It's the art of turning "awkwardly hanging around" into success. They went from customer to coffee clerk, and from coffee clerk to bookseller. From their part-time duties, Gretchen began to collect new responsibilities and new enthusiasms for bookselling. Eventually they took on events, and redoing the website, and an organizing role with local sci-fi convention WisCon. "Somewhere in there I just kind of became full-time," Gretchen explains. Sometime soon after that, Room owner and co-founder Sandi Torkildson began thinking about retiring.

So here's the situation: first-generation feminist bookstore pioneer Sandi Torkildson is ready to retire (Torkildson was the first American Booksellers Association board member from a feminist bookstore); a group of dedicated staff, including Gretchen, is thinking about succession; and the bookstore is going through lean times. Room's future was uncertain. Then, Room's landlord sold their Johnson Street building to developers aiming to knock it down and build a high-rise.

For the first time in Room's history, but not the last, a landlord's decisions forced the store to move. In 2012, Room moved to 315 West Gorham Street downtown, merging with Avol's, the used bookstore that was already in the space. At least one of the booksellers at Avol's, Wes Lukes, stayed on when it became Room. The new location, and the addition of used books, represented a change; Gretchen explains, "We've had to reinvent ourselves a few times." Through all these challenges, Torkildson had to get creative to keep the store afloat. Room ran a campaign urging customers to buy five more books than they'd bought the previous year, because the economic calculations of the new space demanded that much more revenue to stay solvent. The owners also took pay cuts, at various times deferring their own wages to push the store through to the next month. Amid the knowledge that Room's owners were thinking about retiring, some of the staff began to think about what to do next. Gretchen explains, "There was some question of whether we would form a co-op to try and buy it from [Torkildson]. But I had had bad experiences in a co-op . . . I had seen how Sandi had moved the store through pretty lean times. Technically, you can't do [things like wage deferrals] in a co-op." When it came down to it, anyway, there were only two or three Roomers who would be interested in taking over. Not enough for a co-op.

In the midst of these questions and uncertainty, a fateful bookstore event occurred. One day in 2018, *Name of the Wind* author Patrick Rothfuss did an event for one of his books at Room. Gretchen and Rothfuss were acquainted; when *The Name of the Wind* was brand new, long before Rothfuss was famous, Rothfuss met Gretchen at WisCon and handed them a copy of the book. The two literary Wisconsinites remained connected over the years. At the 2018 event, as Gretchen tells it,

> he came down to do an event and was like, "This bookstore is really cool." He hadn't been in the Gorham Street location. He was like, "It's for sale?" And I was like, "Yeah." And he's like, "You're going to buy it." And I was like, "I don't have any money. I've been working *here* for 11 years." And he was like, "Well, I have money, so let me help you." So we worked it out.

Summing up this amazing bit of luck and timing, Gretchen says in a trademark deadpan, "He's a nice guy, and he just really wanted to see us survive." Not long after the event, Gretchen and Wes became the owners of A Room of One's Own with Rothfuss as a silent partner. I wish bookstores like A Room of One's Own didn't need this kind of chain of luck to survive. From uncannily good timing to serendipitous meetings to the whims of generous individuals, there were so many points in Gretchen's story where the chain could easily have broken.

I'm really glad that Room made it through all this. It's truly a special place, a store I look to as a model for my own bookselling practice. The thought of Wisconsin, the Midwest, heck, America without A Room of One's Own is a distressing one. But Room isn't just special because it managed to bust through a difficult past into the present. What makes A Room of One's Own a remarkable bookstore is how it's managing to adapt the original feminist bookstore model into the present moment.

That Gretchen found a home for their nascent queerness at A Room of One's Own is no coincidence. Room and its fellow first-generation feminist bookstore peers were designed as activist spaces where conversations about feminism could flourish. As Kristen Hogan writes in her book *The Feminist Bookstore Movement*, "Feminist bookstores have been not simply spaces to gather but sites of complex conversations among staff and collectives, and, in turn, with readers, about feminist accountability."[27] One of the most important functions of the national network of feminist bookstores was indeed helping people connect and integrate with the feminist movement; as Hogan writes, "In the 1970s, 1980s, and 1990s, women used feminist bookstores as resource centers for finding out what was happening in each city, who had a place to stay to offer to travelers, and where to find a job when they found a city that felt like home."[28] Even Gretchen's transformation from awkward customer to bookseller has precedent in how the feminist bookstore movement functioned, since "the number of women moving through the bookstores as workers suggests that bookstores served as a training ground both for the women working in the bookstores and for those visiting them."[29]

Unfortunately, there aren't that many of these training grounds left. Indeed, the mere fact that A Room of One's Own is still here at all is remarkable. The sad reality is that many of Room's peers from the 1970s have long since closed. For one thing, the 1990s were an incredibly difficult time for bookstores. The peak years of the bookstore mega-chains Borders and Barnes & Noble spelled certain doom for many smaller stores. For another thing, as Kristen Hogan argues, feminist bookstores diluted their message in service of bookstores in general. This dilution happened at the expense of the movement overall, at least according to some. In the 1990s, one strategy that bookstores employed to fight the big chains was litigation. The American Booksellers Association spent much of the 1990s suing big publishers over unfair discounting practices that favored the big chains. This ABA-led effort to correct book industry unfairness led to a politicization of bookstores in general. Many traditional bookstores grew more comfortable taking political stances, beginning with advocating for the importance of small businesses and independent bookstores in particular. But while it represented a radicalization of traditional bookstores, it also represented a diluting of the already-radical feminist bookstore messaging: in large part, the feminist bookstores threw their weight behind advocating for bookstores in general rather than their specific work advancing feminist goals.[30] Indeed, this move towards the mainstream was reflected in feminist bookstores becoming more general-interest in what they carried. Room was no exception. In recent decades, Room has pivoted to add used books and general-interest titles; as Gretchen has explained to *Publishers Weekly*, "In order for Room to survive, it had to be more of a generalist indie bookstore."[31]

Atlanta's Charis Books & More, another surviving first-generation feminist bookstore, maintains a list of currently operating feminist bookstores on their website. The list is 22 stores long. As far as I can tell, 6 were founded in the 1970s. Compare that with Kristen Hogan's claim that there were 130 feminist bookstores at the peak of the movement.[32] Sara Luce Look, Charis's owner, echoes the perception that most original feminist bookstores have closed. She tells me, "In 1994 [when I started at Charis], it was the height of feminist bookstores and I didn't know it, which means there were over 120 in the US and Canada specifically. And then around 2013, there were only around 13 left."

As the idea of feminist bookselling continues to find its footing after the collapse of the feminist bookstore movement, Charis is facing some difficult decisions in how to post and maintain their website's list of feminist bookstores. As Sara explains, in 2023, it's tough to pin down an exact idea of what a feminist bookstore even is:

> When we updated our feminist bookstore list and actually decided to put it out on the internet, we got all these people who said, "I want to be on your list." And [in many cases, a] bookstore is run by feminists certainly, because we're in this moment where feminism is popular, feminist books are popular. Everyone is mission-driven. But we're talking about being mission-driven in a very specific way and about the books that we carry on our shelves and the programs that we do and what we choose to promote and how we hire and how our internal processes work and what we say publicly.

Though Sara and her team at Charis want to honor the legacy of feminist bookstores and the definition of the term, and though they keep a list on their website, they are not interested in being the judge of what is and isn't a feminist bookstore. Sara tells me, succinctly, "I don't actually want to be the gatekeeper." So the definition of "feminist bookstore" in 2023 is in some ways up for grabs as feminist bookselling emerges from the shadow of the classic feminist bookstore movement. Still, there are a few survivors from the original generation. Charis is one of them. So is A Room of One's Own.

Though it has evolved into a general bookstore, in part to be able to survive into the 21st century, Room still maintains a connection to one tenet of the original feminist bookstore movement: the creation of what Hogan calls "the feminist shelf." The feminist shelf is a group of physical and philosophical practices that feminist bookstores employ to, essentially, utilize their bookstore space to make feminist arguments. As Hogan defines it, the feminist shelf is "a complex practice of using spatial organization, programming, and reflection" to do the philosophical work of feminist bookselling.[33] At Charis, Sara tells me, "In Kristen Hogan's book about feminist bookstores, she talks about the feminist shelf. That's what we do. . . . That is the heart of what feminist bookstores do. It's literally about what books you're going to see next to each other and how they are on the shelf together." Indeed, the basic space of Room's store is bursting with signs and signposts to help readers engage with social movement texts. On one recent trip to Room, I saw a staff-picks wall full of queer and anti-racist books, an entire room devoted to a queer fiction section, and a sign bearing a QR code directing patrons to donate to an abortion fund. To wander in Room's new location, a cavernous building with a gorgeous arched wooden roof, is to encounter at every turn feminism, queerness, and what Room refers to as "trans-ecstasy": a bold and proud celebration of all trans people and their stories. One thing Room has mastered is the creation of the shelf as argument for its voice and philosophy. Room has even brought the act of feminist shelfmaking online, where social media expert Fawzy Taylor has created a viral line of flowcharts introducing readers to a broad range of texts from queer, Indigenous, and Latine writers. Example charts include "I wanna read Indigenous writers," "Sad sapphic reads," "I wanna get into queer science fiction," "I wanna get acquainted with small presses," "queer fantasy," and "so you want to read about disability justice." Both online and in person, Room is updating the feminist shelf for 21st-century bookselling.

Room's updated practice of shelfmaking represents a balance between honoring the store's past in the feminist bookstore movement and transforming into something new. As Gretchen tells me,

> I think [about] trying to stay flexible and recognizing that your legacy is your change as well. We are not the same store that we were in 1975, and that's good. And that doesn't mean that what it was in 1975 wasn't crucial and important. It was. And part of honoring a legacy is recognizing the ways in which you hope that what you're doing now is going to be old hat by the time someone takes over from you and that they are going to have the energy and creativity to turn it into something theirs and something new that recognizes the spirit of what you've been trying to do, while not adhering to necessarily the systems of what you were doing.

Indeed, even as Room engages in the practice of creating the feminist shelf, they are updating the work of the feminist booksellers, which Kristen Hogan calls "bookwomen." First of all, Room's predominantly trans or nonbinary staff requires a more expansive term than "bookwomen." For example, Gretchen is nonbinary. Gretchen and Wes initially balked at foregrounding their identities after taking over Room. Gretchen explains to me that they and Wes were "both like, 'If we could avoid being perceived ever, that'd be great.'" But social media coordinator Fawzy "definitely pushed us to brand us as a trans-owned bookstore." Leaning into queer and trans-ecstatic bookselling has allowed Room to find a voice that honors its history as a feminist bookstore while evolving into something new. Gretchen admits that it wasn't a painless transition; part of assuming a trans-ecstatic identity involved "recognizing people [who said], 'I just feel grief over the loss of what we had, this community that we had that no longer exists.'" Indeed,

Gretchen admits, "We were sort of sleeper agents a little bit. I think if the community that supported Room through all those hard times knew like, 'Oh, we're going to turn it into a transapalooza,' they would've been pissed." In response to this pain, Gretchen offers the idea that "what's happening now is [not in] direct opposition to your experience. We want the world to be better for the next generation. We don't want it to be the same. . . . Part of what we're trying to do is just say, 'Hey, we're opening the doors more.'" Sara Luce Look and her team at Charis are also working to invite people into a trans-inclusive practice of feminist bookselling, even if they're facing some similar reluctance. She tells me, "A lot of feminist bookstores got really stuck in their trans politics specifically. . . . The reality for us is that we are still trying to build bridges with a lot of those women that are transphobic." It's not easy work, but both Charis and A Room of One's Own believe broadening their feminism to be trans-inclusive is the future of feminist bookselling.

That door-opening has had an impact. Room has picked up several accolades in recent years, and the awards offer insight into the impact that Room's revamped vision has. When the staff at Room won the prestigious Midwest Bookseller of the Year Award, the award citation described Room as

> a staunch defender of trans rights and a vocal advocate for queer, trans, and BIPOC people everywhere. This commitment to uplifting historically unrepresented communities is present in everything they do—social media, events, custom merchandise, the books they stock and promote—and has been especially uplifting during a year of isolation and political strife.[34]

Later in 2021, Gretchen and Wes won *Publishers Weekly*'s Star Watch Award. In the essay accompanying their nomination, Gretchen is quoted as saying they "have been proud to reinvigorate the store's mission and update it to promote anti-racist activism, prison and police abolition, and trans inclusivity, as well as other forms of progressive politics."[35] This reinvigoration of the store's mission, this promotion of the ideas that mean the most to Room, happens through an updated take on Hogan's concept of the feminist shelf.

To Gretchen, the question of what books to carry is not something to debate in the abstract. They see the arrangement and selection of books in their store as something of vital importance, even as a matter of life and death. They tell me,

> We're seeing more and more clearly over the last two or three years how effective misinformation [can be]. . . . It has killed a million people. And when you say you'll entertain anything [by stocking any book], that means that you are only making the space as safe as the dominant culture is . . . you can't treat people's very reasonable and real threats and fears as just a topic of conversation.

A book's potential to cause harm is one of many reasons Gretchen may choose to include or not include it on Room's feminist shelf. They tell me:

> There are thousands of books I don't carry in my store. And some of them are just because I don't hear about them, and maybe I would. Some of them are because I just don't think they're that good. And some are because I think that they are ideologically dangerous.

This curation is a key part of the feminist shelf and has been part of feminist bookselling for a long time. One feminist bookseller quoted in *The Feminist Bookstore Movement* explains "the difference between censorship and buying decisions" by stating that "we make buying decisions every day and buy the work we want to promote and don't buy things that are in conflict with our values." Hogan calls this framework "a necessary refining of bookwomen's ethical relationality."[36] Ultimately, Gretchen agrees with their feminist bookselling forebears that this isn't a free speech issue at all. The First Amendment protects speech from the government, not from independent bookstores. As Gretchen explains, "Me not carrying [a book] in my one bookstore in Madison, Wisconsin, does not mean that that information is not accessible to somebody who wants it."

Ultimately, to Gretchen, the question of shelfmaking is more than a theoretical debate reserved for tweets and the opinion pages of *Publishers Weekly*. What's in their store, and by extension what their store stands for, "matters to me. It matters to my wife. It matters to my trans kid. Our living experience here matters." The queer-inclusive feminist shelfmaking at Room is much more than curation or experiment; it's a reflection of the values and experience of the people who work there. How can a store build a diverse and welcoming environment for booksellers and readers if it's promoting books that debate those people's very right to exist? What kind of bookseller would work in that environment? What kind of queer reader would shop there? And what kind of bookstore could build a future without a diverse and welcomed core of booksellers and readers?

The booksellers of Room, and the moves that Gretchen has taken to empower and protect them, are another crucial element of their queer-inclusive bookselling practice. While the feminist bookstore movement was laudably dedicated to advancing the feminist movement, Gretchen is committed to justice work *and* protecting the workers doing it. The first thing Gretchen says when I ask how to ensure a good future for bookstores is this:

> Make sure you're investing in your staff. I hear anecdotally how hard that is for some people to do. Like, I hear from other booksellers that are really chafing under their ownerships not paying them enough. But we try to give bonuses when we can. We try to give raises when we can. We try to prioritize staff happiness and security when we can. And we can't do it for

everyone in every situation. I try not to overpromise, and I try not to under-serve as much as possible.

It's refreshing to hear a business owner, not to mention a bookstore owner, talk this way. Especially after my years of researching Amazon and how it does things, I celebrate Gretchen and other business owners like them who can say, as Gretchen did, that "the old systems of trying to extract as much efficiency from your workers as possible are not sustainable." One reason these systems are not sustainable is how fraught and occasionally dangerous bookselling work can be. As Gretchen explained in a recent staff meeting, "We're going to be a target because we're openly progressive, openly queer, openly trans, and that's getting scarier and scarier." But at every turn, Gretchen and Wes empower and protect Room's booksellers to whatever degree they can, telling them,

> I'll have your back. I trust you to make the kindest and most protective of yourself and of the business decisions as you can. You're not children. You're not idiots. You know what you're doing. You are a self-possessed person, and your personhood is important, and you deserve to work somewhere where you aren't getting demeaned by people.

A good future for bookstores is a future where more bookstore owners talk like this.

Through worker-friendly bookselling and a queer and trans-ecstatic update on traditional feminist bookstore practices, A Room of One's Own is emerging into the 21st century while many of its original peers have closed. A core part of their success is an acceptance of change and its possibilities. Gretchen tells me, "Look, we are doing what feels important to us now. Are we always going to be expressing things the exact same way? No, because we are human beings who learn and change, and I hope that we can continue to learn and change as we progress." Ultimately, Room's day-to-day guiding principles might not even be centered on the question of "how can feminist bookselling be updated for a trans-inclusive future?" In fact, that might be *my* question. Instead, it ultimately seems like, in Gretchen's words, Room is "just trying to find what needs our community [has] and how are we able to fill that need in, like, capitalism." And even if many of Room's booksellers "don't actually want to be working in capitalism . . . asking people to move their money around in a more just way is, I think, a reasonable thing to do."

· · ·

In many ways, the story of A Room of One's Own is a story about the highs and lows of being a bookseller. With Gretchen and Wes, Room has an ownership team that's dedicated to empowering booksellers in as many ways as possible, from welcoming all kinds of queer identities to offering the highest wages possible in this pinched industry. To talk to Gretchen is to hear a boss who thinks of their workers first, and I think the quality of the bookselling experience at Room speaks to that empowerment. But Room, being openly queer and abolitionist in a heated political climate, is by necessity also a dangerous place to work. This kind of outspoken advocacy is being met more and more with vitriol, threats, and hatred from the right. This will only increase as the right continues their culture war against queer books. Members of bookstore communities should take steps to protect booksellers and the work they do.

## ACTION STEP: DO WHAT'S GOOD FOR THE BOOKSELLERS

For all the Silicon Valley whizbangery that goes into a Kindle, or Amazon's search algorithm, or any number of other attempts to techify bookselling, tech bros have yet to invent anything that's better at selling books than an actual human. The shelfmaking that is practiced at places like A Room of One's Own or Charis is a human practice; no computer could match a human's ability to turn a bookstore's physical space into a powerful point of view. The same can be said for the human-to-human conversational art of book recommendation, which booksellers commonly call "handselling." Josh Cook, veteran bookseller at Massachusetts's Porter Square Books, has published a delightful and detailed chapbook explaining his philosophy of handselling. In it, Cook writes that a book recommendation is

> like a spark of electricity leaping across a synapse. . . . When a reader leaps across that fundamental gap by taking a risk on a book I recommend, we share something beyond an exchange of information: faith in the ability of people to share something whether they know anything about each other or not. And when a reader loves a book I recommended to them, that risk and faith are rewarded with meaningful connection. Recommendation algorithms attempt to erase this gap.[37]

All this isn't to say digital shelfmaking or handselling is impossible; it is to say that only a talented human could make a flowchart introducing readers to great queer books like Room's Fawzy Taylor did throughout 2022. Only a human could curate a jubilant, trans-ecstatic display like the ones dotted throughout Room's maze of queer literary joy. Only a human can lead a reader into a bookstore and send them on their way with a delightful and unexpected recommendation. The clearest evidence of this is the failure of Amazon's physical bookstores: their shelfmaking was by algorithm, not the human mind, and the resulting spaces were sterile, unwelcoming, and bizarre. Amazon shuttered the entire failed experiment of their brick-and-mortar bookstores in early 2022.

Shelfmaking, or even just a good book recommendation, is a bit of magic. There's a lot that goes into it. A reader won't want something exactly like the last book they read, because that'll be boring. You can only recommend the same author until the reader reads all that author's books. People love to be surprised, but there are lots of bad ways to be surprised—a lover of sweet rom-coms may be surprised by the thoughtful gore in a novel by Stephen Graham Jones, but not necessarily in a good way. But then again, the right romance reader might actually pounce on a good horror book. It's impossible for a computer to know. It's difficult for even a human to know, but certainly not impossible, especially if that human is a clever bookseller. Any given bookstore is likely filled with several of these clever booksellers, and watching them do their work is a thrill that will enrich your reading life. At the Raven, a lot of the booksellers have "fans" that follow all of their recommendations. Literally as I write this, a Raven colleague just texted me: a customer came in to say the last seven books they read were all staff picks from the same bookseller.

As a member of a bookstore's community, it's easy and beneficial to participate in this. Just walk into a store and talk to a bookseller. Or call the store. Or email them. However you do it, ask them for a recommendation. Recommendation-seeking protects bookstores because it's job security: the more people take advantage of recommending, our most important skill and one that cannot be digitally replaced, the more demand there is for our services. That hopefully turns into sales, of course, but it also turns into more perceived value for what we do. Publishers, authors, and other book industry folks will notice and appreciate the skill and value of our work, which will go a long way towards ensuring our future.

Increasingly, though, those talented human booksellers have a lot more than books to worry about. Since March 2020, countless public health enforcement decisions have fallen on hourly retail and service employees. For the last three years, every bookseller in the country has been in countless arguments about masks and vaccines. These conversations are not easy. I myself have been threatened (by a handwritten certified-mail letter, no less) because of my store's mask mandate.

Even without these post-2020 difficulties, bookstore work has always been hard. If you've been in retail or service, you know it. Long hours on your feet. Difficult customers. Getting stuck in the weeds when the store is super busy. Physical pain. Mental exhaustion. I once heard someone say that a US senator couldn't make it through a single peak shift at a Starbucks, and I believe it.

And of course, as discussed elsewhere, all of this happens while nobody doing it is making much money.

Yet we still do it. We have our reasons, from love to economic necessity to loyalty to stubbornness. But regardless of why a person happens to be working in a bookstore (or any retail or service environment), they are deserving of patience and respect. Here's what keeps booksellers going: when someone is kind or welcoming or interesting or fun, this job is worth it, despite its difficulties. One of the job's biggest rewards is the satisfaction of good interactions with kind and respectful customers. To protect bookstores, protect the dignity of those who work in them.

The most obvious way to do this is to pay them more. Now you may think I'm arguing two different things when I say both "bookstores don't make enough money" and "minimum wage should go up." But, as I've said elsewhere, a bookstore's best investment is the people that work there. Some bookstores, like Room, increase wages voluntarily. The Raven's starting wage is well more than double the federal minimum wage, for instance, and we do everything we can to ensure employees are at or above the living wage for our county. But being able to guarantee that any job, bookstore or otherwise, pays a living wage is one way for government to protect small businesses. Researchers at UC Berkeley have found that "a higher minimum wage can produce benefits not just for workers, but for their employers, their communities and the entire economy."[38] After all, raising compensation for all workers means people will have more money to spend at small businesses in their communities, like bookstores. Raising the minimum wage would be a step towards embracing the radical notion that people who work at bookstores should be able to afford to shop at them.

# CHAPTER 4:
# "THIS ACCUMULATION OF HISTORIES"

## Shakespeare and Company, Paris, FR

S hakespeare and Company, on Rue de la Bûcherie in Paris, is the world's most Instagram-worthy bookstore. There's only one problem: photos aren't allowed inside. There are signs saying as much everywhere in the warren of rooms, nooks, and surprises that collectively form the bookstore that's operated across the Seine from Notre-Dame since 1951. After you wait in line to get in, you'll see a sign that says "no photos" at eye level right in front of you, next to a big display of *Shakespeare and Company, Paris: A History of the Rag & Bone Shop of the Heart*, the magnificent 2016 book that the bookstore published about its history. You'll see signs that say "no photos" tucked into shelves. Next to the mirror at the top of the stairs, decorated with scraps of paper bearing little messages that people have taped up, you'll see another "no photos" sign. And you'll see yet another one propped up in the typewriter in the Sylvia Beach Memorial Library, the hushed and sacred room at the end of the store's second floor whose job is to house the book collection of George Whitman, founder of the second Shakespeare and Company, while honoring Sylvia Beach, founder of the first. In addition to "no photos," this particular sign says, "Please respect our readers and writers," suggesting that taking photos in this bookstore is somehow detrimental to reading and writing. The sign might have a point. Of course, people take photos. Tourists pose in front of bookshelves, and people sneak videos as their partners hack out

Coldplay songs on the piano (the piano's sign: "PLEASE PLAY QUIETLY"). But, as far as Paris tourist attractions go, there are far fewer phones held aloft here than there are at, say, one of this city's excellent art museums. During my time in Paris, I saw people rushing through the impressionist gallery at the Musée d'Orsay, just casually snapping a picture of every painting without even pausing to look. I saw people trying to make tracking shots of the entirety of Monet's immersive 360-degree water lilies at the Musée de l'Orangerie. Here at Shakespeare and Company, though, people are just as likely to sit in silence as they are to filter what they see through their screen. Many don't even read. They just quietly absorb the space, feeling the history of this bookstore. It's not hard to do.

This bookstore is the second bookstore in Paris to bear the name Shakespeare and Company. The first, famously, was founded by Sylvia Beach in 1919. Beach, an American who decided to stay in Paris after volunteering in the Red Cross during World War I, ran her Shakespeare and Company not only as a bookstore but as a gathering place for the group of writers now known as "the Lost Generation." For these authors—Hemingway, Fitzgerald, Stein, Joyce, and Pound among them—"she operated as banker, post office, clipping service, and cheering section."[39] The original Shakespeare and Company also acted as a publisher: in 1922 Beach decided to publish James Joyce's monumental *Ulysses* herself, after no publisher dared touch the allegedly "obscene" book. Every time a bookseller advocates for a book that the mainstream won't touch, or every time a bookseller takes a stand for free speech, they can look to Sylvia Beach's efforts to publish *Ulysses* as an early example of how bookselling and advocacy are intertwined. And her advocacy efforts were vigorous. Every copy of *Ulysses* that Beach sent to the United States was confiscated. So she worked with Ernest Hemingway to find someone to smuggle copies across the Canadian border one at a time. She continued her vital and inspiring efforts until the economic devastation of the Nazi occupation shuttered her store.

Just a few years later, after extensive vagabonding around the world, an eccentric character named George Whitman arrived in Paris. Whitman was a former American soldier and an outspoken socialist with odd habits; never one for a traditional haircut, he was known to simply light his hair on fire when it got too long. A decade after the Nazi occupation ended Beach's version of Shakespeare and Company, Whitman began trading his food rations for book rations and hoarding books in a dingy, condemned storefront immediately across the Seine from Notre-Dame in the Latin Quarter. This roughshod stockpile would later turn into a charming, threadbare bookstore. Among Whitman's customers was none other than Sylvia Beach. Eventually, Beach became so enamored with Whitman's operation that she ceremonially bestowed the Shakespeare and Company name onto it. Like Beach's incarnation, Whitman's Shakespeare and Company was also much more than a place to sell books. Indeed, the selling of books was often secondary to Whitman's main goals. His version of the store was more like a freewheeling boarding house than a traditional retail operation. Whitman's Shakespeare and Company was a lending library where visiting writers could stay the night for free as long as they helped with the store and left a bit of writing about their experience for the archives. These visitors were called Tumbleweeds. It's not uncommon to hear a story about a wandering traveler appearing in Shakespeare and Company only for Whitman to hand them the keys and take off to parts unknown; commonly, these folks ended up staying there for months at a time. Tumbleweeds can still stay at Shakespeare and Company in exchange for labor and writing to this day. In this way, the store became a hub for generations of writers, travelers, and thinkers in Paris.

When describing his work, Whitman used language from radical social movements, certainly not accidentally. Of his more-than-a-store, he said, "This is my commune . . . I like to think the bookstore is part of an archipelago of utopias that stretch across the world from Costa Rica to Kathmandu . . . for miles along the Seine River, this is the only door that is open to strangers every day of the year from noon to midnight."[40] I asked his daughter, Sylvia Whitman—who runs the bookshop today—to articulate what exactly the Shakespeare and Company philosophy is, and she replied in kind. She described George's bookselling philosophy (and, by extension, hers) as "a socialist way of thinking: give what you can, take what you need. He was always very emphatic. He was like, 'This is not your shop. You share it with everyone else and you always have an open door and it's there to be shared. You are looking after it, but you share it with others.'"

Further cementing his store's point of view, George Whitman's mission of communal hospitality became crucial during moments of social upheaval. During the Paris student protests of 1968, "the bookshop was a refuge. George hosted all-night talk sessions, and he hid those who were trying to escape" the police.[41] A few years later, the *Houston Post* would write that Shakespeare and Company offered "a meeting place for any cause dedicated to human rights and freedom, with no questions asked." [42] In providing this kind of connecting space for potential changemakers, Whitman was pioneering the work that bookstores like A Room of One's Own or Red Emma's (profiled in the next chapter) are doing today. Indeed, Whitman's brand of activist bookselling quickly made the leap to our shores, as it's easy to see parallels between Whitman's work and Lawrence Ferlinghetti's. Ferlinghetti, a close friend of Whitman's, founded City Lights Bookstore in San Francisco in 1953, two years after Whitman got his start. Like his Parisian counterparts, Ferlinghetti created a cozy meeting place for generations of writers and radicals. Like Beach, Ferlinghetti got caught up in legal issues publishing groundbreaking literature that authorities deemed obscene, as the fight over Allen Ginsberg's *Howl* dragged through the judicial system and the court of public opinion. The two stores are spiritually linked: a small blue sign over the front door at Shakespeare and Company reads "City Lights Books." When Sylvia was preparing to inherit the store from George, she spent a week shadowing the booksellers at City Lights to learn the trade. Sylvia tells me that George and Lawrence were so close in their friendship and their bookselling that "at the beginning they were going to swap bookshops every six months." Over the years, City Lights even pondered taking over Shakespeare and Company outright, but to this day they simply remain literary comrades in pursuit of feisty bookselling and bookmaking on either side of the ocean.

When I visit Shakespeare and Company in March 2023, the legend of George Whitman and Lawrence Ferlinghetti still animates the store. Upstairs in the Sylvia Beach Memorial Library, people leaf through George's books. The message he painted above the stairs—"be not inhospitable to strangers, lest they be angels in disguise"—still hovers over countless readers and tourists. And the team behind Shakespeare and Company is taking me to lunch at George and Lawrence's favorite spot, Brasserie Balzar. It's a joy to spend a few amiable hours with these fine literary folks, including Sylvia herself, as well as literary director Adam Biles and head buyer Linda Fallon. The waiters are obsequious in their black vests and bowties as they scoot a table out so we can slide onto the yellow velvet banquette—I get the feeling I'm far from the first writer they've taken to Balzar.

The first thing Sylvia tells me is a story. Once, after one of their regular meals here, George, Sylvia, and Lawrence shuffled into the crooked, cobblestone Latin Quarter streets back to the bookstore. Lawrence looked down and said, "George! You only have one shoe!" George suddenly realized that he'd left one shoe under the Balzar table. He asked Sylvia to go back and retrieve it. She hurried back and discreetly told the maître d' that George had left his shoe under a table. It's worth pausing here to describe the maître d' at Balzar: short, bald, and imposing, he has a gigantic moustache with pronounced curls at either end, and he lords over the bustling space like a king. He doesn't stand. He looms. Immediately after Sylvia whispered to him about the shoe, the maître d' boomed out, "QUELQU'UN A-T-IL VU UNE CHAUSSURE?" hushing the buzzing lunchtime crowd. One table sheepishly raised their hands and Sylvia went to retrieve the shoe on hands and knees from between their legs. "It was covered in maple syrup," she tells me, adding that, like all of George's footwear, he had plucked it from a trash bin somewhere. Quickly, blushing, she snagged the stinking shoe and shuffled out the door.

In many ways, the story represents the professional relationship between George and Sylvia, whose bookselling careers overlapped for a few amicable but tumultuous years before she took over the store following George's death in 2011. One of my favorite stories from the Shakespeare and Company book is George's protest over Sylvia installing an actual, modern cash register. Until that day, cash and transactions were tracked by hand via George's inscrutable handwritten accounting ledger. George responded to the mechanized invader by stealing it. Sylvia tells me, "He was so deadpan with me. He was like, 'Syl, we've had a thief.' And I was like, 'God, who can it be? It's so weird because nothing is broken. It had to be someone who had the key.' When I figured out it was him, I was like, 'That rascal played me so badly.'" But, in hindsight, it seems like George, in his rascally way, was just testing Sylvia. Literary director Adam agrees, saying to Sylvia across the white tablecloth, "So many of your stories from when you first started taking over the bookshop, do you feel like George was testing your mettle?

And clearly being happy with the result of these tests?" Sylvia replies in the affirmative.

Modernizing Shakespeare and Company was always going to be a monstrous task, and it's ongoing to this day. The store is in the midst of never-ending construction that they simply call, in English, "the works." Perhaps "the works" is why, when I ask about what it takes to modernize an iconic but aging bookstore, the talk turns first to construction. I was thinking more philosophically, but Sylvia's answer starts with, "We have to do a lot of the boring stuff, like make the stairs secure, so there isn't, like, a ladder instead of stairs." For sure, a big part of bringing Shakespeare and Company into the 21st century is physical: when a bookstore operates in a space like this, physical stewardship is certainly part of permanence. Fun fact: the building was condemned when George bought it in 1951. Still, he went through with the purchase, saying, "I almost didn't take it when I learned that the building had been condemned . . . but then I found out it had been condemned in 1870, so I decided to take a chance on its holding up for a few more decades."[43] His approach to preservation was always more scattershot than Sylvia's "youthful pragmatism," as Adam puts it—Sylvia tells me that when she took over the store, she discovered the carpet was adhered to the floor with "old pancake batter." George indeed hated the new stairs. As our food arrives, Adam recounts a story of interviewing George and Sylvia for a travel magazine before he started working at the store. He interviewed George first, and the subject quickly turned to Sylvia's new staircase. According to Adam, George said, "Oh, my daughter, she has just replaced the stairs. There was nothing wrong with them, no one fell down them in 50 years. And then now the place looks like Chicago." Later, when interviewing Sylvia—which is when they first met—he mustered up the courage to ask her about her father's disapproval of the stairs. Her first response was, "What's wrong with Chicago?" and her second was, after a huge eye roll, "The police said they were going to close us down if we didn't [replace the rickety old stairs]."

But, of course, the act of bringing a legendary bookstore into the 21st century isn't just physical. George's business model— if you could even call it a business—isn't built for longevity. The store came close to closing several times, and for a few years in the 1960s, visa trouble meant George couldn't sell books at all. If Shakespeare and Company, under Sylvia's watch, was to gain any kind of steady permanence, there was work to be done. The work was both physical and, let's say, metaphysical. Sylvia tells me, "I'm always interested in getting the balance between modernizing it but keeping the soul and the spirit." Delicate work, but it has to be done. Adam tells the lunch group, "For so many reasons, not just for the way people's mentalities have changed and the way regulations have changed, the way economies have changed, it would be impossible to run a place like George ran it in the 1950s. But the question is how do you keep as much as you can about that welcoming open philosophy within a viable 21st-century bookshop?" It's a loaded question, and probably one that animates a lot of backstage discussions at Shakespeare and Company. The answer, at least as Adam, Linda, and Sylvia have calculated it, is to operate in the space between bookstore and museum. Scratch that—there's no space between the two at Shakespeare and Company. It's a bookstore and a museum at the same time, and it's also not quite either. Sylvia has the data to prove it. She tells us that a friend of the store ran a study of how people use the space, and roughly half treated it like a bookstore, with the other half treating it as a museum. A museum of what? Well, according to Adam, a lot of things. He says,

> I think one of the things that appeals to visitors is the layers of the different histories. You feel like you're getting a sense of old Paris and old France. And then you start getting into the literary history. So obviously

it's a different bookshop to Sylvia Beach's, but there's this connection to expat American writers, and then they tap into the history of this specific bookshop, and George's space, and from 1951 onwards, when you had Allen Ginsberg and Burroughs spending time here, and all of the people who've been here over the years, all of the Tumbleweeds who have come as 17-year-olds and then gone on to make amazing movies, or write amazing books, or do things like that. Visitors come for that sense of the accumulation of histories.

The challenge, of course, is to not become a museum outright. Shakespeare and Company is actively resisting that, for what it's worth, and they're determined to function as an actual bookstore even while they honor the "accumulation of histories." Sylvia tells me about visiting a conference in Porto, home to the Instagram-famous bookstore Livraria Lello. To deal with the museum/bookstore/crowd problem they share with Shakespeare and Company, Livraria Lello has started selling tickets to their space. This idea is unconscionable to the Shakespeare and Company team. Sylvia says, "That for me is impossible to do. It goes against the whole ethos of George and Sylvia Beach. I couldn't charge for tickets." So they implement other measures to keep the space functioning as a bookstore—limiting capacity, banning photos, and rotating the staff so nobody is in a high-pressure tourist situation for too long. According to Adam, it's working. He looks across the table to tell Sylvia, "Over the last few years since you've been running the place, I think you and Linda have made it a functioning 21st-century bookstore, which has preserved and brought to the fore this history as well." At Shakespeare and Company, honoring the past and bookselling for today are always happening side by side.

In fact, if you ask Shakespeare and Company, the past and present bookstore work aren't even two different things. It's all part of the store's work, and how it's connected to people over the years. Any idea that Sylvia has swooped in and made a bunch of changes is false, since it was always already evolving since day one. George always had the ambitions that are now being realized—he wanted to take over the whole block. Now, under Sylvia's watch, there's a café that stretches the Shakespeare and Company presence all the way to the corner of Rue Saint-Julien le Pauvre. He dreamed up the balcony that Sylvia and her partner David just engineered into life. Adam explains this continuity well when he says, "The bookshop was constantly changing from the very first day. And it's not like there was a George version of the bookshop [and a Sylvia version]." Perhaps that's why nothing is under glass in the Shakespeare and Company museum/bookstore: it's because the past never ended here. It bleeds into the present, and honoring both is part of the store's future. You can touch the past. People do. Sylvia tells me that visitors "come in and they'll touch the beams, because they could see how much history there is and how old the building is." Some go beyond mere touch, choosing to leave their mark on the space. Every Tumbleweed who sleeps on the beds scattered throughout the rooms is required to write a one-page memoir for the archives. Upstairs, there's a typewriter and a stack of paper you can use. Never mind that the typewriter doesn't work. Perhaps it's out of ink. Or perhaps it's designed to type ghost letters. Down the hall, at the top of the "Chicago" stairs, there's a mirror over a Tumbleweed bed where people have taped little scraps of paper with messages. Hundreds of them. Here's a sampling:

- "In love with this pleas"

- "De Bilboa para el mundo"

- "I love you, Sylvia"

- "Leer te lleva mucho más allá que los sueños."

- "I don't know if you ever got here, but you would've loved it."

- (every word is in Chinese except "Paris")

- "I'm Isabella. I'm here with Emma and Rose (they don't know I'm writing this) and I feel so alive for the first time in a while, so thank you for that."

- "Volvemos pronto"

- "This is a perfect place."

- "We are here."

- "Nice bookshop where time and place become irrelevant."

Shakespeare and Company is and isn't a museum. It is and isn't a modern bookstore. You can touch things and write on the walls. There are no plaques explaining the history because all you need to do to see history is look around, or maybe touch a beam. To stand in Shakespeare and Company is to stand at the very intersection of the past and the present.

Something about the mission is working, because people are flocking to Shakespeare and Company by the thousands. Sylvia estimates that they get between 2,000 and 3,000 visitors a day, and there's often a line to get inside. The store is very crowded, especially on the bottom level where the new books are for sale. But though none of the books in George's second-floor library are for sale, Sylvia's friend who did the space-use study says 30% of the people in the bookstore go upstairs anyway. They go upstairs to sit, to snuggle on a Tumbleweed bed, to read, to think, to soak in the immaculate vibes of one of Paris's most significant literary rooms. And Sylvia hopes she can hook those people on bookstores in general. It's not hard to imagine that many of those thousands of visitors don't patronize their bookstores back home. Sylvia wants to change that. She tells me, "I feel this privilege of being an independent bookshop that seems to be on people's list to come and visit. We get a lot of people. And a lot of those people don't go to their independent bookshops at home. And so it feels a bit like a showcase. I feel like we need to show how cool independent bookshops are, and then convert people to independent bookshops." I can think of one case where it worked: I first went to Shakespeare and Company on my honeymoon in 2013, and a year later I got a part-time job at the Raven.

I'll never forget that first visit to Shakespeare and Company. It was my first time overseas, and my first time in a country that didn't speak English. I was having a rough time with that. I didn't prepare nearly enough, and every time I ordered a meal or tried to buy something it felt like an ordeal. I was jet-lagged and frustrated and wondering if the whole trip was a very expensive mistake. I had heard that I should visit Shakespeare and Company, but I didn't know anything about it. So after we wandered around in the majestic gothic dark of Notre-Dame, we walked across the Seine and into the bookstore behind the green façade. Immediately, a cheerful bookseller cried a friendly "hello" and I was flooded with relief. I remember the book I bought and the happy hour spent in there and the feeling of that place. This was before the TikTok era, so the no-photos thing wasn't even an issue yet. I don't think I even had an Instagram. So I was surprised and a little put off on my second visit, a decade later, to find a queue out front and people sneaking photos inside, not to mention just how busy the store was. In my memory—which I'm sure is false—my wife and I were the only people in there. This is normal for such a wonderful space. People build very personal connections to it, and that makes them feel a sense of ownership. When discussing the store's evolution, Adam tells me, "For everybody, the perfect incarnation of the bookshop was when they were there." When he says this, I feel called out. So when I return once again to the store the day after lunch at Balzar, I try to let go of my rosy memory of 2013 and allow myself to feel something new. As I wander the crowded rooms, I think of the Monet paintings I saw at the Musée d'Orsay that morning: Five views of the Rouen Cathedral in different lighting. Two views of the same Japanese garden bridge. Some variations on the same haystacks. It can be rewarding to return to a subject, but only if you let yourself see it a bit differently each time. A bookstore can encourage this, can't it? Perhaps, a bookstore even forces it—the nature of a bookstore is that you can never step into the same bookstore twice. Especially one that's constantly evolving, like Shakespeare and Company. It forces the visitor to see the same place in a different way.

My experiment works. I am much more able to feel the magic of this place when I let go of my nostalgia for my first visit. I feel reverence in the Sylvia Beach Memorial Library. I feel awe in finding a whole shelf of vintage green Penguin Classics. I could stay in here for hours. I'm not even reading. I'm just watching the parade of browsers and feeling the weight of history. If you ask me, my sense of presence owes a lot to the space itself and to those no-photos signs. There are interesting things to look at, both book and non-book, from the floor to the ceiling. You can't walk in a straight line for more than a few seconds, a fact that requires you to be present in your surroundings lest you literally bump into one of those ancient beams. And because I squashed my (admittedly very strong) impulse to document my experience in real time, I could *feel* my experience in real time. In this way, Shakespeare and Company is doing a third thing, in addition to honoring the past and being a bookstore in the present: they're forcing people to *be* present.

When I ask her about the no-photos signs, Sylvia says she doesn't mind if people take photos, really. But she adds that a bookstore like Shakespeare and Company "can put forward values that are maybe being forgotten or being put aside. We can say, 'Come in, take a break from your phone. Not everything has to be online.' I always quote this Lewis Buzbee line from his book about bookshops, where he says, 'This wonderful, charming combination of solitude and gathering that independent bookshops provide,' it's so good." I think of my visit the previous day to Monet's staggering double 360-degree Nymphéas installation at the Musée de l'Orangerie. A sign outside the exhibit explained Monet's thinking about its design. With no way to know the rooms would one day be stuffed with people making TikToks and taking selfies, Monet said that "those with nerves exhausted by work would relax there, following the restful example of those still waters, and to whoever entered it, the room would provide a refuge of peaceful meditation." The same can be said about Shakespeare and Company, or really any bookstore, if you're willing to pay close enough attention.

• • •

In one of our several conversations during my time in Paris, I mention to Sylvia Whitman that there is seemingly a bookstore on every block in the Latin Quarter, the neighborhood Shakespeare and Company has called home for 72 years. She replies, almost casually: "Yeah, there's over a thousand in Paris." I'm left speechless. By comparison, similarly sized Chicago has roughly 55 bookstores.[++] Linda, the Shakespeare and Company head buyer, chimes in to say that there are over 150 in the fifth arrondissement alone, an area of one square mile with a population of 60,000. That's like having 150 bookstores in Eau Claire, Wisconsin. Whichever way you shake it, bookstores are far more abundant (and long-lasting) in France than they are in the United States, and that kind of thing doesn't happen by accident. France's thriving bookstore scene is the result of decades of policy specifically designed to protect bookstores.

# ACTION STEP: POLICY TO PROTECT BOOKSTORES

Several countries in Europe have laws that limit the discounts retailers can put on books. These laws protect bookstores because they prevent chains and large retailers—and now, places like Amazon—from engaging in predatory pricing that would squeeze smaller bookstores out of the market. It's a forced leveling of the playing field. In the US, superstores and Amazon can use their massive scale and varied revenue sources to allow them to sell steeply discounted books as loss leaders. Of course, small bookstores can't do that. But in parts of Europe, nobody can put steep discounts on books, regardless of the retailer's size or scope. These policies are explicitly designed to protect bookstores, and they're working.

The first fixed-price book law in Europe was France's.[45] The law, widely known as the Lang Law, was spearheaded by former culture minister Jack Lang and signed into effect in 1981 by Socialist president François Mitterand. Until 1979, French publishers and booksellers had voluntary agreements limiting discounts and protecting small bookstores. Then, in 1979, Economy Minister René Monory made a decree that these agreements were illegal. Big French bookstore chains like Fnac then made quick work of implementing predatory discounts. To further understand the Lang Law and its legacy, I shared a cup of coffee on the plaza outside Shakespeare and Company with Laura de Heredia, staff member at French bookstore union Syndicat de la Librairie Française (SLF). According to Laura, with no fixed-price agreements, Fnac and chains like it "were beginning to take a lot of market share, so booksellers were beginning to have some real difficulties." Mitterand and his Socialist Party made it part of their 1981 platform to repeal such decrees and protect small bookstores. Mitterand was sworn in as president in May 1981; he immediately asked Lang to come up with a fixed-price book law. The Lang Law passed unanimously in August of that year. To this day, under the Lang Law, no retailer can discount a French book more than 5%. Coming from the United States, I'm fairly shocked to see such a law implemented so quickly and lasting so long. I ask my new French bookselling friends about it, and they bring it back to the idea that French people value bookstores as part of their culture, as part of what makes France French. Laura from SLF tells me that the Lang Law passed because of the "defense of values for French culture." Adam from Shakespeare and Company tells me that "the French, in certain ways, know what is good about their country and value it and are ready to protect it, whether that be the cultivation and production of wine, or cheeses, or bread, or bookshops in a town."

The Lang Law isn't the only French policy designed to protect bookstores. In March 2023, when I spoke to Laura from SLF, a law requiring a minimum shipping cost for books had been passed but not implemented yet. So, she told me, Amazon and companies like it could legally get away with charging one cent for shipping. Part of the delay is that now, unlike in 1981, policies like this need approval from the EU in Brussels. Since we've talked, though, the law has been finalized: Starting in October 2023, books will carry a minimum shipping cost of 3 Euros on orders up to 35 Euros.[46] This doesn't make anybody 100% happy: big French chains like Fnac were hoping for 2 Euros, and bookstores, claiming the cost of shipping a book is actually around 6 Euros, were hoping for 4.50. Still, at least some French booksellers are excited: I learned that the law had been finalized via an email from Sylvia Whitman saying, in part, "Hurrah for these French actions—it's a real inspiration."

According to Laura from SLF, the French government was quite active in making sure bookstores made it through the pandemic, too. For one thing, books were declared essential, allowing bookstores to stay open through the various lockdowns. Laura tells me that at one point, the government even covered shipping costs for all orders through bookstores. During France's second lockdown, she tells me, "The Ministère de la Culture said that they would suport booksellers, and so they took care of all shipping costs from booksellers. For two months, we could ship for free to customers."

Regardless of what exactly the policy looks like, France is a clear example that policy can work as a way to protect bookstores. It's the biggest difference between the bookstore scene in the US and the bookstore scene in France. In the early 1980s, as France was passing a strong policy specifically designed to protect bookstores, the US government was busy gutting antitrust enforcement (more on that soon). This is perhaps the biggest reason a French city of two million people can have almost 20 times as many bookstores as a similarly sized American city. The Lang Law worked. It continues to work. Surely it's one of the reasons a place like Shakespeare and Company has found such longevity—seven decades of eccentric, self-described socialist bookselling, thanks to French bookstore policy. The official Shakespeare and Company memoir says, "In August of [1981], Mitterand's government passed the Lang Law . . . the result was that France had—and continues to have—one of the strongest, most diverse bookshop cultures in the world."[47] But you don't have to read the book on Shakespeare and Company to credit their longevity, and the success of all of France's bookstores, to the Lang Law. You can just ask them, and over our lunch, I do. Here's the exchange:

Me: Is the Lang Law why France has so many bookstores?

Sylvia: Yes, definitely.

# ACTION STEP: WALKABLE, PEDESTRIAN-FRIENDLY URBAN DEVELOPMENT

The Lang Law is perhaps the single strongest piece of policy that has protected French bookstores. But it's far from the only one; many more general political decisions in France and Paris have protected the city's thousand bookstores. For one thing, France is a pedestrian-friendly city. Small businesses regularly thrive in neighborhoods where it's easy for folks to get around without a car; a bookstore or other small business can sink or swim based on sidewalk traffic. But pedestrian-friendliness doesn't happen on its own. It requires political involvement and smart decisions about how a city is developed. Paris has miles and miles of protected bike lanes, an extensive Metro and bus system, and a general culture that's focused on the sidewalk rather than on the highway. The end result is a city of two million that can support a thousand bookstores. Compare that to American cities, especially smaller cities away from the coasts. In the 1970s and 1980s, shopping malls pulled commercial and pedestrian traffic away from downtowns and towards the highway-dotted outskirts. That problem was compounded as Amazon warehouses pulled even more jobs and commercial activity away from urban centers. The end result was development focused on cars, and American downtowns that could no longer support bookstores and small businesses. Sure, fixed-price policy is good for bookstores, but so is policy that works to keep pedestrians and economic activity downtown.

In researching this book, and talking to people about the Lang Law and France's support of bookstores, I often got the question, "Do you think a Lang Law could ever happen in the United States?" It's a difficult question; I'm an optimist at heart, so I don't want to say no outright, but there are days when it seems like a stretch. After all, one of the things that allowed for Lang to write and implement his law was the fact that he was a cabinet minister for a Socialist president. The odds of *that* happening in the United States certainly seem slim right now. But I don't want that to discourage people from pushing for policy that protects bookstores, small businesses, and vibrant, pedestrian-friendly urban cores. After all, there's a lot more that can be done towards those goals besides federal policy. Many development decisions happen at the municipal level, where a room full of citizens raising their voices can have significant sway. The Raven is located on Massachusetts Street in Lawrence, Kansas, a commercial district that has faced challenges but has largely retained a small-business-centered vibrancy. This is because the people of Lawrence value Mass Street's character, and they show up to fight for it whenever developers threaten to permanently alter it. There are many points in Lawrence's history when a room full of concerned citizens have successfully persuaded city government to side with historic preservation and small business over the interests of developers.[48] That's where policy starts: in local rooms with local citizens raising their voices. If national policy seems like too steep a goal, start by pushing for bookstore-friendly urban development in your own community.

# CHAPTER 5:
# "HOW TO TURN INFORMATION INTO A WEAPON IN THE FIGHT FOR A BETTER WORLD"

## Red Emma's Bookstore Coffeehouse, Baltimore, MD

*T*he first thing that Cullen Nawalkowsky tells me is that he's not an anarchist. He's a veteran bookseller, a longtime participant in the leftist scene, and one of the folks responsible for shaping the book inventory at Red Emma's Bookstore Coffeehouse, a landmark cooperatively owned bookstore in Baltimore. But, he's not an anarchist. He explains, "I always have to make sure to assert that. The amount of times I've seen the phrase 'self-described anarchist' or 'so-called anarchist,' when I've never called myself one." He laughs and continues, "Certainly some of the other founders of Red Emma's are anarchists and define themselves that way. We are obviously named after an anarchist. We're inspired by anarchism. We do events for anarchists, all those things. But we've never defined ourselves as an anarchist bookstore." Indeed, at least according to Cullen, Red Emma's is designed as a space for political work by everyone working for a just world, and even more, a space to bring all those folks together, anarchist or not.

Cullen and I are talking over coffees at the new Red Emma's building in Baltimore's Waverly neighborhood. On the street level it's a vast but cozy coffee shop serving ethically sourced coffee drinks and vegan food. Exposed brick and a gigantic RED EMMA'S sign line one wall; the floors are shiny concrete. Hushed conversations happen at tables and overstuffed leather armchairs. Downstairs is a low-ceilinged and cramped bookstore space, a temporary home for the book side of Red Emma's while they finish renovating the other of the two adjacent buildings the co-op just purchased.

For Red Emma's, the journey to this permanent home in Waverly was a long one. The founders of the co-op met in the early 2000s at meetings and actions organized by an anarchist bookstore called Black Planet. When describing Black Planet, Cullen says, "I won't call it nonprofit because that's actually a legal designation. It just didn't make any money." Eventually, according to Cullen, the store's owner "got over his head with stuff" and the store became a collective which Cullen joined. After Black Planet closed in 2003, a few people from the collective began to think of next steps. At that time, Cullen says "it seemed like the sky was really falling" in the bookstore world. That made the Black Planet folks think about other ways to make a sustainable attempt at continuing their radical bookselling work. So, according to Cullen, they thought, "Let's also make it a social space. How about a coffee shop? Because similarly, the coffee world was not where it is right now. Honestly, there weren't a lot of coffee shops in Baltimore." There was a need in Baltimore for both a radical bookstore and a good coffee shop, so why not try to do both? Cullen explains,

> All those ideas went together and drove us to reinvent what was Black Planet Books and turn it into Red Emma's. But we wanted to be a lot more serious about our institutionalization and building structures regarding roles and accountability and things. Just trying to figure out a way to become more defined as an organization and ideally to produce good wages

to be able to be a platform for other organizing that's happening in the city and regionally.

Eventually, they arrived at the concept of Red Emma's Bookstore Coffeehouse. According to the "about us" page on the Red Emma's website, they "wanted to both establish a firmer financial foundation to keep the new project afloat, but also to create a more welcoming environment." The site goes on to list the twofold Red Emma's mission statement: "first, to demonstrate, concretely, that it's possible to build institutions that directly put values like sustainability and democracy to work, and second, in doing so, to build a resource for movements for social justice here in Baltimore."

Red Emma's achieves the first part of its mission by operating as an employee-owned cooperative. Setting this up was no joke, requiring the navigation of a tangle of legal and other obstacles. For one thing, in Maryland, business owners technically have to file taxes quarterly instead of annually. For another thing, the Red Emma's founders didn't want to saddle the value of the inventory onto the workers' tax burden. Eventually, Cullen tells me,

> we had to create a legal structure where the worker owners are owners, but we are also employees. So everybody who gets money is an employee and gets paid as an employee and can just file and just pay taxes as once a year, your standard taxes. But then the worker owners are also the board, and then the board makes the decisions.

According to this system, it is also possible to be an employee without being an owner. Initially, the co-op tried making everyone an owner, but that got too difficult. "A lot of things went wrong with that," Cullen says. But the possibility of working at Red Emma's without being an owner hasn't decreased engagement or interest in ownership. He tells me that "currently, everybody who is working here is on the path to being a worker owner." As Cullen explains, an employee works towards becoming an owner by staffing the bookstore or coffee shop and attending some training sessions "around collective decision making, around accounting, things of that nature, the history of the organization, et cetera." After four to six months, usually, the owners decide whether a worker is ready to become an owner based on a vote. The whole thing is a democratic process, by design. More importantly, it's also a path to business ownership that doesn't require an investment of capital, vital in an industry where few people make enough money to become business owners in more traditional ways.

As Cullen tells it, Red Emma's didn't arrive at their co-op ownership structure overnight. The current well-established cooperative model is the result of many years of trial and error. The same can be said of the physical home of Red Emma's. This building, newly purchased by the cooperative, represents the third time Red Emma's has moved in their roughly 20-year history. Of course, the purchase of the building is aimed to create a more permanent and lasting space. But the cooperative was also intent on picking the right permanent space. As Cullen tells me, "The specific move that we made to this specific location was motivated by a desire to be more situated in a neighborhood." He tells me Waverly has a rich history with social justice causes: "And All People's Congress was right around the corner. There was a free health clinic nearby. The Catholic Left of Baltimore was very close by. There's a lot of deep left history going back at least half a century in this neighborhood. And that was also part of the appeal for us."

Picking a neighborhood is one thing, but being able to purchase a building is quite another. How did a radical employee-owned cooperative—not the type of operation known for being flush with cash—swing it? By cashing in on 15 years of hard work and goodwill. As Cullen explains it,

You generate goodwill over time. And the people that you've built up goodwill with are all of a sudden sitting on a board somewhere, or they know somebody, or they know how they can get you something. It's just building that over the years and living our values in a way that people recognize and say, "Actually they're legit about what they say they're about, and they also are legit about operating something. They're not going to run away." So we've got our radical connections, and then we've got our more above-ground business connections. And ironically, the pandemic sort of helped because there was two years where we didn't really have to worry about, "Is enough money coming in so that we can pay wages?" Because we were able to get PPPs, there were other grants that were available to small businesses, and we had 15 years behind us, so we would be . . . high on the list of people to get these grants and get these loans.

A website dedicated to the store's Waverly move lists specific support from places like Central Baltimore Partnership, Central Baltimore Future Fund, the Baltimore Roundtable for Economic Democracy, Seed Commons, Waverly Main Street, the Maryland Department of Housing and Community Development, and Baltimore Regional Neighborhood Initiative. For a group like this to purchase their building and create a permanent home for their work is no small feat. From listening to Cullen talk about it, and reading how they describe it online, it's apparent that they worked very hard and with great pride on the move. Red Emma's has spent more than a decade building connections in Baltimore justice circles, and those connections have made it possible for them to create a permanent home.

Permanence is the key idea behind a radical space like Red Emma's. In buying their building and creating a lasting space for their work, Red Emma's is fully taking advantage of one of the vital aspects of a radical bookstore in comparison to other movement spaces. A protest, as a counter example, is a movement space for a few hours before it reverts to being an intersection or plaza. An occupation can welcome people into social movements for a few days or weeks until it's cleared out. But a radical bookstore, especially one that's thoughtfully creating a permanent home in a building they own, is constructing a much more durable movement space. As Kimberly Kinder writes in her book *The Radical Bookstore*, "Instead of borrowing other people's spaces or relying on other people's patronage, retailing generates an independent source of income to pay for independent spaces where activists can make independent choices."[49] Of course, radical retail represents something of a trade-off, since "securing this independence comes at the price of capitulating enough to external market and government forces to stay in business, which involves compromise instead of outright resistance."[50] But, even if creating this durable space requires an unsexy reliance on compromise in lieu of revolution, it can be worth it: "the benefit, when it works, is enhanced autonomy within a durable space under activist control."[51] In creating a sustainable business model and in purchasing their building, Red Emma's is striving for a rare thing: an activist-controlled space, where activists have full autonomy, on a permanent basis.

Since the outset, one of the store's goals in creating their permanent activist space has been building connections on the political left. That goal is reflected right there in the second half of their mission statement, which pledges "to build a resource for movements for social justice here in Baltimore." This broad mission is one of the reasons Cullen told me not to call him an anarchist—though Red Emma's has goals that include anarchist practices and ideals, their aims are broader than that. As Cullen tells me between bites of his salad, "One of the things that we were really excited about doing is having more broad radical space that wasn't necessarily strictly anarchist or punk or counterculture, though we wanted those things to still remain. We recognized that there's people who are in other radical traditions like Pan-Africanism, socialism, and even Democratic Socialists or Social Democrats." This broad view of social justice movements, and what Red Emma's could do to foster their work, was in part inspired by the desire to avoid siloed thinking. According to Cullen, "We weren't explicitly anarchist or explicitly communist or explicitly this or that because we would find people really shut themselves off and would sometimes discuss ideas without actually relating to them." Entrenching yourself in one specific mode of thought isn't the Red Emma's way; rather, their goal is to give a home to all kinds of voices, creating connections and possibilities for a better world. This isn't to silence anyone, but rather to further social change by building connections. Cullen tells me that this refusal to identify with any one specific movement is not meant

> to trump somebody, it's to deepen their understanding
> of the various forms of control, oppression, domination,
> life, et cetera, that exist. No one theory and one approach
> is going to get you all the way. We just always try to
> recognize that, while understanding that we are also an
> above-ground commercial institution that has its own
> limitations and can only do so much. As such, we want
> to give the space for people who are doing other types
> of activity to learn, connect, et cetera.

In setting up their bookstore with this philosophical bent, Red Emma's is taking inspiration from the infoshop movement. As the Red Emma's website defines it, an infoshop is a place that exists to "provide points of distribution for viewpoints and information that could never get a hearing in mainstream media and bookstores." In doing so, "the physical presence of an infoshop can help pop 'filter bubbles,' exposing people to new ideas . . . above all help[ing] to bring people together to dream and scheme on how to turn information into a weapon in the fight for a better world." For the kind of radical folks who run a place like Red Emma's, the idea of selling things and participating in retail commerce can feel like a compromise, sure. But don't let that obscure the fact that what they're selling—radical information that doesn't get a fair airing in the mainstream—is also a key part of the way they work to build connections and fight for a better world.

Another word that can be used to describe this infoshop-inspired method of building political connections is "triangulation." In *The Radical Bookstore*, Kimberly Kinder paraphrases writer William H. Whyte's definition of triangulation, saying it "occurs when something in the environment—such as a food vendor, art installation, or cultural event—generates an excuse for strangers to chat without having to introduce themselves or disclose personal information."[52] The books, the coffee, the whole infoshop atmosphere at Red Emma's create an environment for political connection through triangulation. It's an inclusive (and, dare I say, hopeful) view of political bookselling. Red Emma's doesn't exist just to sell radical books to already-radical people. They aim to build connections and welcome people to social movements. The goal in creating this community is inviting people in, expanding the movements for social justice. As the Red Emma's website says, "There's no point, after all, in a space dedicated to spreading radical information if the only people who ever come in are already radicalized!"

Aside from providing space and fostering connections through triangulation, another way Red Emma's hopes to foster social change is by proving that the co-op model actually works. That's the motivation behind creating durable systems and an above-ground business that functions not only as a co-op but also as a viable money-making enterprise. Cullen says part of the inspiration for Red Emma's was wondering, "How can we conceptualize something that is scalable? Even though we're micro, can we grow that? Or if not, can we build an institution in a way that other people want to model? Then, can we relate to one another and build a cooperative economy as time goes on?" This is work that Red Emma's takes seriously; I suspect it's one reason why Cullen was ready to talk to me so enthusiastically for this project. Other co-op members have put in real work trying to spread the cooperative model in Baltimore and beyond. Most notably, as explained in a *Baltimore Sun* article, Red Emma's co-founder Kate Khatib "is also executive director of the Baltimore Roundtable for Economic Democracy." The *Sun* explains that "BRED has helped other area businesses transition into worker-owned cooperative models, whereby employees can own part of the business and have a say in how it's run. North Avenue pizza shop Joe Squared recently announced it would transition to a worker-owned model."[53] Presumably, Red Emma's has a lot of reasons for operating as an employee-owned cooperative. Of course, they believe in a democratic workplace where all co-op members are owners of equal shares in the business. But they don't seem content to simply build one co-op, as they work to help their egalitarian model spread in Baltimore and beyond.

As I've researched Red Emma's and listened to Cullen, I've been struck by the pride that the store takes in what it does. Just because the staff are radical activists doesn't mean they're not good at selling books. Just because profit and wealth generation aren't their goals doesn't mean they're not excellent salespeople and coffee roasters. It's evident as soon as you step into Red Emma's: the books are thoughtfully curated and the people who sell them firmly believe that curating and selling them is working towards making the world a better place. The coffee is delicious and lovingly roasted and sourced. The food is creative and tasty and vegan. Even though there's an element of compromise involved, creating a space like Red Emma's to sell books really can advance radical causes. According to Kimberly Kinder, "Although shopping is often dismissed as a passive, frivolous activity, constructing counterspaces in the guise of storefronts creates low-stakes environments for search and discovery."[54] The books aren't simply something that gets in the way of doing the real work. The books are part of the work, and Red Emma's is good at it. As their website says,

> We want to show that anarchism doesn't mean being disorganized and that anticapitalism doesn't mean being unable to operate effectively and efficiently. If you've ever had to defend your conviction that the world would be a better place without bosses asking hostile questions about who would take out the trash and who would scrub the toilets, you can point to Red Emma's and win your argument. No bosses and no hierarchy, but we've been taking out the trash, ordering books, running a restaurant, dealing with the accounting, and a thousand other things for the better part of a decade.

This all shows that there are different ways to create a great bookstore and community space. As Cullen tells me, "those of us who started this, we were habituates of bookstores and coffee shops and stuff like that. And so wanting to preserve and represent that magic to new generations of people is something that we aspire to do." If Red Emma's is to be believed (and they should be believed), that magic is possible outside of traditional single-owner or single-boss models.

Occasionally, when talking to other folks about radical bookstores and what they represent, I've been met with skepticism. One radical friend of mine seemed dismissive of the whole thing, saying in essence that a worker-owned business is still a business. If revolution is the goal, is selling things part of the struggle at all? Employee ownership is still ownership, right? I understand where he's coming from, but it's hard not to be inspired by sitting in a place like Red Emma's and hearing its folks talk about their inclusive and idealistic view of what a space like this can do. I ask Cullen about the possibilities for revolution and his answer is a characteristic mix of pragmatism and inspiration. He tells me,

> To me, whether you're optimistic or pessimistic about the prospects of large-scale social change, it makes sense to develop different types of institutions and begin working in them and through them and creating practices and learning whether or not we're going to fully transform society. If we do fully transform society, we need some experience. If we're going to turn a large sector of the population into cooperatives, we need people to have experience working in cooperatives. If we're not going to have a large-scale social transformation, it makes sense to carve out as much space as possible with different types of social relationships and different types of economic foundations.

The revolution, if it comes, may very well start with conversations in a place like Red Emma's. And even if the revolution never comes, Red Emma's and places like it are doing important work imagining different possibilities.

•     •     •

Many of the bookstores in this book are making individual efforts to create good workplaces; for instance, Avid protected their queer booksellers by cancelling the second day of a school book fair after a parent challenged a queer book. Additionally, A Room of One's Own makes a lot of small-scale efforts to do what they can to raise wages and protect their workers. But a core argument of this book is that individual efforts won't solve systemic problems. While these efforts by individual stores are vital and worthy of celebration in their communities, systemic solutions are required for the systemic problem of book industry labor concerns. Red Emma's approaches this challenge by working to build exportable systems for worker-owned co-ops and advocating for their adoption in Baltimore and nationwide. To protect bookstores, this kind of systemic protection of booksellers (and all low-wage and/or hourly workers) is necessary.

# ACTION STEP: SYSTEMS AND POLICIES THAT EMPOWER WORKERS

Not all bookstores prioritize worker empowerment. Some bookstores, facing unionization efforts, have declined to voluntarily recognize the unions or have even engaged in unionbusting tactics. Some bookstore owners might argue that unionizing is too expensive, because higher wages would cut into the oft-discussed thin margins. They say that involving a union prevents direct communication between management and rank-and-file employees. These folks would probably argue that protecting the right to unionize is in fact the opposite of protecting bookstores.

I disagree. If there's no future for workers in bookstores to engage in well-compensated, rewarding, safe work, then there's no future for bookstores. Here's what I mean: if people can't make decent careers as booksellers, then bookstores will suffer. A bookstore with empowered, well-compensated employees is a bookstore built for the future. A bookstore that can't retain talented people is doomed to an endless cycle of hiring, training, and dealing with employees who aren't particularly dedicated to the store or bookstores in general. Red Emma's has an inspiring answer to this: offer booksellers an ownership stake in the business. As owners, they'll be more invested in the business, and ideally they'll have the chance to earn more money by claiming their share of the business's profits. But Red Emma's is one store, and the vast majority of bookstores are not worker owned. An entire industry built on low wages, long hours, and high turnover is a house of cards waiting to collapse in the slightest breeze.

It follows that one way to protect booksellers—and, in turn, bookstores—is by legally protecting things like worker-owned cooperatives and unions. Imagine if there was an easy legal pathway for forming an employee-owned co-op, rather than the legal tangle Red Emma's had to fight through for years to land on their business model. This is why their efforts to create a scalable, exportable model for employee-owned cooperatives are so important. When the Raven was exploring employee ownership in 2021 and 2022, we kept running into options that required tens of thousands of dollars in legal fees, simply out of reach for a business like ours. Another legal obstacle for workers is so-called "right-to-work" laws, which aim to strip unions of their power.

But there's hope for worker-friendly legislation: in the 2022 midterm elections, Illinois voters easily added a workers' rights amendment to the state constitution, and in early 2023 Michigan became the first state in 50 years to repeal a right-to-work law.[55] Union activity also appears to be on the rise in the US. The past few years have featured some amazing union-formation successes. For example, hundreds of unions have formed at Starbucks stores nationwide. And, stunningly, in April 2022 the JFK8 Amazon Fulfillment Center on Staten Island successfully unionized with the startup Amazon Labor Union.

Despite the recent wave of union activity, the book industry has a disproportionately low level of unionization. Still, there are a few unions who represent different kinds of book workers. The HarperCollins Union is the only union at a Big Five publisher, and independent leftist press Verso is unionized. Other unionized publishers include the New Press, Duke University Press, and Harvard University Press. A small but increasing number of bookstores are unionized, including Politics and Prose (Washington, DC), Solid State Books (Washington, DC), Greenlight Bookstore (Brooklyn), the Strand (New York City), Powell's Books (Portland, Oregon), Page 1 Books (Albuquerque),

Skylight Books (Los Angeles), Moe's Books (Berkeley), Green Apple Books (San Francisco), Bookshop Santa Cruz (Santa Cruz), McNally Jackson (New York City), Book Culture (New York City), BookPeople (Austin), the Savoy Bookshop (Westerly, Rhode Island), and The Elliot Bay Book Company (Seattle). Workers at these places have decided that forming a union is one way to address the systematic challenges facing book industry workers.

Of course, forming a union is just a first step. Companies like Amazon and Starbucks (and perhaps some bookstores) might delay, resist, and otherwise filibuster the contract process through legal maneuvering, endless appeals to the National Labor Relations Board, and other unionbusting tactics. This isn't hypothetical: as I write this, unionized employees at Big Five publisher HarperCollins have just returned to work after 60 days on strike, the longest strike in HarperCollins history. The strike allowed them to win a contract including many of their demands for higher pay and union protections. But the benefits of the new contract expand beyond HarperCollins: writing for Vice News, Claire Woodcock claims that "the agreement has the potential to drive union organizing within the publishing industry."[56] The thing that eventually broke the stalemate and helped secure that contract? A federal mediator. The government can and should be there to help unions deal with corporate anti-union behavior. A fair and equitable union contract means security for a bookstore, because properly compensated employees who feel safe and seen at work are the best investment a bookstore can make in its future. One way the government can help ensure a good future for bookstores, then, is to interpret and enforce labor law in a way that protects even the smallest of unions from even the most ruthless of unionbusting campaigns.

But you don't have to be a policymaker to support labor unions and their right to advocate for their members. During their months-long strike, the HarperCollins Union widely circulated a list of steps that readers, authors, and booksellers could take to help support their efforts. They asked agents to hold off on sending pitches to HarperCollins editors. They asked booksellers to distribute bookmarks printed with union-supporting designs. They asked readers to post the union's graphics to their social media. All of these small steps are nonetheless steps towards ensuring a good future for workers in the book industry. (One important note is to always check whether the union is calling for a boycott or not; the HarperCollins Union expressly asked folks not to boycott, as a boycott could have helped management make the case that the union was bad for business. The best thing to do is subscribe to unions' social media or email newsletters and follow their lead in taking small steps to protecting a worker-friendly book industry.) In a piece about bookstore unions for *Teen Vogue*, Kim Kelly quotes Tove Holmberg, a veteran unionized bookseller at Powell's Books in Portland, Oregon, as saying, "Book workers, like all workers, deserve to have a voice in their workplace, and the most powerful voice is the collective voice of a union."[57] Ultimately, Kelly comes to the conclusion that to support books, it is necessary to support the people who make and sell them: "If you love books, show love to the people who make them possible—and support their efforts to organize."[58]

# CHAPTER 6:
# "A NEW BATTLE EVERY YEAR"

## Bookends & Beginnings, Evanston, IL

*T*he day I visited Nina Barrett, owner of Bookends & Beginnings in the Chicago suburb of Evanston, I had breakfast with my good friend Paula. Paula and I went to undergrad together. Before that, she grew up in Evanston in a historic house not far from Bookends & Beginnings' spot in an alley downtown.

That day, Paula and I had breakfast burritos and a companionable chat, catching up. By the time breakfast ended, I still had 45 minutes until my meeting at Bookends. Paula and I decided to walk over to the library, which Paula said was lovely. After discovering that the library was closed, we ended up just walking slowly around downtown Evanston. This was fine with me; as previously discussed, I have a well-documented affinity for college towns, especially their downtown small business districts like the one we were roaming. As we walked, Paula told me everything that had changed since her childhood. She listed businesses that were gone: over there was a Barnes & Noble, which shut down a few years ago. Over there was Dixie Kitchen, a soul food place Barack Obama loved. Here's the Urban Outfitters, now empty. Like other Urban Outfitters locations, they had decals on the doors that made the glass look shattered. Mannequins and fixtures sprouted dust inside. More and more as we walked, it seemed that Paula's childhood happened at places that were closed or gone.

One Evanston landmark that survived, albeit in evolved form, is the low-slung cinderblock building tucked away in an alley behind Evanston's Sherman Avenue. For decades, the building housed Bookman's Alley, a dusty and cramped but beloved bookstore. Now, Nina Barrett and her team have reinvented the space as Bookends & Beginnings. Low-ceilinged and creaky-floored, the building doesn't even have plumbing (the bathroom is in a space across the alley that B&B has been using as a stationery and sidelines shop). Bookends is the kind of shabby old building that, as a bookstore, emanates warmth and welcomes you in. A series of connected rooms, it pleasantly encourages browsing and lingering. I thoroughly enjoy my time browsing there, but I also can't stop thinking that it's not an ideal bookstore location. It's not visible from the main drag. When arriving, I wasn't even sure I was at the right place until a bookseller ushered me in. Nina had all this to deal with when she started her business, plus the long shadow of the beloved bookstore that occupied the building for decades before hers arrived. Still, she's a fighter, so resurrecting and reinventing this hidden bookstore was an effort she was willing to make.

When I ask her about the changes Paula told me about that morning, Nina says, "It's a battle for the soul of Evanston." Indeed, Nina's fight involves her bookstore, but it's bigger than that. She tells me, "It isn't just about bookstores. It's about your whole downtown community. It's about the shoe store that isn't here anymore and the stationery store that isn't here anymore." She tells me just this morning she heard a restaurant called Found was closing up shop. Found opened at the same time as Bookends & Beginnings and Nina felt "a kinship with this restaurant. . . . It had this very indie restaurant vibe, while most restaurants here are very slick. I read this morning that they're leaving, they're closing because there is a development planned for their building." We're sitting at a table in the back room at Bookends & Beginnings, in the shadow of a massive receiving desk, and though Nina looks a bit crestfallen, passion animates her eyes. To her, empty storefronts represent more than an eyesore:

We talk about empty storefronts as if they're just an aesthetic problem, as if it's acne, but let's add up all of the missing sales tax from all of the businesses that are not there. You know why they're not there paying sales tax? It's because we have a landlord issue where the landlords won't negotiate to a market price that would be affordable for anybody who's trying to sell enough stuff to pay their rent.

It's easy to respond to this by saying a commercial lease isn't a public concern, it's a private negotiation between two private parties. But to Nina, it is public: this kind of landlord-tenant conflict "isn't a private matter because ultimately if you wind up with a downtown that has no small business in it, it's not private anymore." If small businesses can't make it, it's a civic problem. After all, policymakers tacitly acknowledge this when they give subsidies to large-scale developers who promise economic activity. But such aid for small businesses is harder to come by: Nina tells me, "We need our value in the community to be reflected in dollars. We just do. They do that with developers all the time. So why can't they do that with us?"

Mind you, restaurants are closing everywhere. Businesses don't last forever. But, according to Nina, the reason the empty-storefront problem is a battle for the soul of Evanston is that the businesses swooping in to replace the closing independent shops make Evanston seem like any other town. The developers that are buying up buildings and land, forcing out small businesses in Evanston, lean towards national, established brands instead of local shops. Nina argues that "if [a town] has a Starbucks and it has three T-Mobile stores and six nail salons and a lot of empty storefronts," there's nothing to distinguish it from other towns. What kind of business is well known for countering this, for giving a town a unique flavor? A bookstore, of course. Nina tells me (and I'm inclined to agree) that the businesses "that make people feel that they've *been somewhere* when they go to that town, often that's an indie bookstore. And we're being challenged on so many different fronts with very little civic recognition or certainly financial support for what we're bringing to the table."

Nina would know. In the days leading up to my arrival in Evanston, Nina got a letter from her brand-new landlord informing her that her rent was going up by 125%. Nina's building is changing hands, you see, and is now owned by a developer who wants to "revitalize" the alley that Bookends & Beginnings calls home, christening it "Bookman's Alley." He promises cafés and outdoor seating and all kinds of little improvements. In the landlord's eyes, these improvements will increase Nina's business and that's enough to justify more than doubling her rent. As we talk in a quiet corner of that very building, Nina wonders aloud why anyone would create a development named to suggest the presence of a bookstore and then saddle the resident bookstore with an unaffordable rent. Unsurprisingly, she's furious. After all, there seem to be different developer rules for large businesses versus small ones. Nina explains,

> Every time Amazon says they're going to open a new warehouse, there are subsidies and incentives. I'm sorry, but if we're going to be your flagship business anchoring Bookman's Alley with a bookstore, you're doing the opposite to me of what happens [to Amazon]. Instead of getting incentives and rewards for being what you're selling to the public, you're penalizing me with an extra $30,000 worth of rent.

Unfortunately, there's little Nina can do. Still, one thing is for sure: it's not her first fight. She tells me, "I feel like there have been a number of different battles that we have fought here, basically a new one every year." And Nina won't back down from any of them.

Nina, a journalist and author, spent part of her early career moonlighting at Chicago's Women & Children First, a first-generation feminist bookstore that Nina calls an "intellectual candy store." "I didn't realize it at the time," she tells me, "but I was learning how a bookstore runs and I was having access to the intellectual richness that a bookstore is and how a bookstore is important in its community." Many years later, Nina heard of an opportunity in Evanston. Throughout her time in the near-north suburb of Chicago, Nina had wondered why there wasn't a "funky college bookstore" in a town that could clearly support it. Part of that was probably the Borders and Barnes & Noble superstores fighting each other for customers downtown while Bookman's Alley slowly spent decades selling used books in cramped confines in its quiet alley. By the time Bookman's Alley closed in 2013, Borders was gone and Barnes & Noble looked pretty hobbled (the Evanston B&N did end up closing in 2020). Nina sensed an opportunity, and she didn't even share my misgivings about the location: "This space represents the perfect location, the perfect atmosphere. And it's like the demographic of Evanston is the demographic that you would invent to support the kind of bookstore I always imagined could flourish here. So I thought it was worth taking the chance." Nina cleaned up the building a bit, reinventing the space as Bookends & Beginnings, a source for new books rather than antique ones, but retaining touches like vintage rugs and furniture that had given so much charm to the old Bookman's Alley store. Slowly at first, she worked to build the bookstore she knew Evanston needed. And now, nine years later, it's still here.

Despite all her battles, Nina believes in selling books. Where other booksellers might have qualms about participating in a capitalist system, Nina tells me, "I don't have a problem with being a merchant. I don't have a problem with being a for-profit store. I don't think there is an existential problem with that." When I bring up the idea that perhaps the commercial for-profit model might not be a perfect way to value everything that a bookstore can do, Nina responds forcefully: "I am not running a museum here, and I'm not running a library, and I don't want to be a not-for-profit. I want to make money so I can pay decent salaries and health insurance and all those things to the staff who are the people who keep it running every day." I don't think Nina is a capitalist, especially since the first thing she says she'd do with any money that comes from her store is pay her workers. Rather, I think Nina believes in commerce. Nina has a good idea for a business, and she wants that business to make money so she can pay her employees and contribute to the economic activity in the hometown she loves. "I don't think that bookstores are dead," she declares. "And I don't think we're not viable. I think we are viable, but we need to stick up for ourselves." That's exactly what Nina does whenever obstacles impact the viability of her bookstore. The problem isn't the bookstore, the problem is the systemic forces getting in its way. When those forces, like misguided developers and greedy landlords, do get in the way, it's battle time: Nina tells me, "I think we should speak up to those forces and I think we should fight those forces. . . . My position is I would rather sue Amazon and I would rather agitate with city government to say, 'What are you going to end up with at the end of this? Isn't this a problem that we all need to solve together?'" And lest you underestimate the fight in Nina, she's not kidding about suing Amazon.

Indeed, in the spring of 2021, Nina Barrett, represented by Steve Berman and his law firm Hagens Berman Sobol Shapiro LLP, as well as the Chicago-based firm Sperling & Slater, sued Amazon. Basically, the class-action lawsuit alleges that Amazon and the Big Five publishers conspired to control book prices in a way that makes it impossible for small bookstores to compete. According to the complaint, filed in the United States District Court for the Southern District of New York,

> Amazon and the Big Five restrain competition in the
> sale of print trade books through highly restrictive

most favored nation clauses (MFNs) in their distribution agreements. These anticompetitive provisions ensure that no rival bookseller can differentiate itself from, or otherwise compete with, Amazon on price or product availability in the sale of print trade books.

The suit alleges that Amazon is the center of a hub-and-spoke price-fixing conspiracy with the major publishers. The allegations resemble a successful suit previously brought against Apple for fixing the prices on ebooks. According to the allegations in the Amazon suit, Amazon separately negotiates similar contracts with each of the major publishers, securing discriminatory list price discounts only available to Amazon and fixing prices in the greater book market. Further, the suit alleges that Amazon is fixing prices by lowering prices for Amazon while also raising prices for other bookstores and consumers. Even without the discounts, the mechanics of the bookstore model and the publishing industry in general make it very difficult for bookstores to lower prices to match Amazon. In short, the suit alleges that the contracts between Amazon and the Big Five make it impossible for anyone else to fairly compete with Amazon. If the suit progresses, the idea is to consider all bookstores who ordered books from the Big Five a class eligible for compensation. To Nina, it's not even that outlandish of an idea. She tells me, "I'm astonished Amazon hasn't been sued more." And while she acknowledges that any suit against Amazon is an uphill battle, she says, "I think the lawsuit will force some of [Amazon's] financial practices into the open. Maybe it will force some kind of remediation of these financial practices. Maybe if it goes forward, the people in the class will get some money back, and what's wrong with that? Because there's no doubt that we have all suffered financially from Amazon's business practices. If there's a payoff in the end, that seems fair to me, in the light of all the damage that has been done to our industry."

As this book goes to print, Nina's current battles are ongoing. The lawsuit has slogged along. In its initial form, it was dismissed by a magistrate judge. Basically, it was found that the major publishers all had different enough contracts with Amazon that they were considered to have been negotiated in good faith to meet competition from the other publishers, rather than being part of a hub-and-spoke price-fixing conspiracy. Further, the plaintiffs didn't actually claim that the publishers had directly communicated about the alleged hub-and-spoke agreement. Part of the reason why the ebook price-fixing suit against Apple was successful was because the publishers were proved to have communicated about the scheme. Though Nina's Amazon suit was revised and refiled, a second motion to dismiss is pending at the time of this writing. Even if Nina's suit fails, I think there's something to be admired in her willingness to be the public face of such actions. A reinvigorated antitrust movement is a key part of building a world where bookstores can thrive, and legal fights like this are part of that goal. And while, understandably, many people have a hard time getting fired up about the complexities of antitrust law, they'll connect with these issues a lot more if they see how their beloved neighborhood bookstores are being affected.

Nina's other battle, with the landlord's 125% rent hike, escalated much more quickly. While she got both the mayor and her alderman to speak to the new landlord on her behalf, he refused to negotiate a new lease. So Nina decided that Bookends would have to move, and fast. The timeframe for finding a new storefront, cleaning out the old one, preparing the new one, and moving all the fixtures and books ended up being about six weeks. They had to vacate the alley building by the end of January 2023, and rent would start being charged on the new building in February. For reference, the Raven took more than a full year to find, renovate, and move to a new location. On top of that, Nina was hospitalized for three herniated discs between

Christmas and New Year's 2022. All told, Nina's effort to move Bookends fast would be herculean, and she would need help.

She appealed to the city to help fund the relocation with a grant from the $43 million it had received through the American Rescue Plan Act (ARPA) but was informed by the city that she was not considered eligible for ARPA funding. The city did agree to allocate $83,000 from other sources, and this is certainly a big deal. Government support for bookstores at any level is very hard to come by, and Nina managed to secure quite a bit. Still, the $83,000 in city money represented only about 18–20% of her total projected costs for moving and building out the new space. On top of that, she didn't know how fast the allocated money would come through, and her expenses were immediate. So she turned to GoFundMe, raising more than $110,000. It was still short of the total cost of the task at hand, and as of this writing Nina is still seeking donations and still lobbying the city for ARPA funding. Still, even being able to raise $190,000 and moving a bookstore in six short weeks is evidence of the amount of fight in Nina. So is this fact: The last day at the alley location was January 28, 2023. On February 15, Nina and her team held a soft opening in the new space, inviting the 1,400 GoFundMe donors. And despite fighting through what many would consider a bookstore owner's worst nightmare, Nina didn't lose touch with the joy of bookselling. In a note to donors announcing the soft opening, Nina promised that the new space is "completely magical in its own way." She sums up her feelings for the whole ordeal in a text message she sent me, saying, "Our new store is gorgeous and we are already getting a ton more walk-in traffic. So, kind of an improbable ending to what could have been a dark story—and is for so many stores."

•    •    •

Nina's battles, like any bookstore's battles, are both global and local. This probably rings true for a lot of booksellers. I spend a lot of time worrying about both Amazon and the fact that the Raven's back door is shifting in a way that makes it hard to lock. I read news articles about Amazon's latest corporate misdeeds, and I also read my lease to see whether I'm on the hook for a new door, or if my landlord will pay for it. It's just the nature of the job; global and local concerns collide, and nobody demonstrates that more than Nina Barrett fighting Amazon and fighting to find a new space at the same time. In that spirit, this chapter's action steps are a mix of policy suggestions to deal with Amazon, and immediate ways to protect bookstores in crisis.

## ACTION STEP: ADDRESS THE AMAZON PROBLEM

Amazon remains the biggest roadblock to the success of all retail small businesses, including bookstores. This is true because of their massive market share in everything from shoes to books to video camera doorbells, and their anticompetitive tactics in those markets. In discussing her lawsuit, Nina says the hub-and-spoke allegations aren't the thing that bugs her most about Amazon, but rather what her lawyers see as Amazon's legal liabilities. If you ask a bookseller what does bug them about Amazon, they'd probably say predatory pricing. Amazon heavily discounts retail goods, forcing their competitors out of business. Then, they slowly raise prices. This is common monopoly behavior, and it's not particularly legal, but it's very rarely prosecuted; one antitrust lawyer I spoke with said that bringing a predatory pricing case is "impossible." This is why Nina's lawsuit doesn't go after Amazon for predatory pricing, where it harms bookstores the most. Rather, Nina's lawyers apparently believe price fixing and claims of price discrimination—brought under a rarely enforced 1936 federal statute known as the Robinson-Patman Act—are where Amazon is vulnerable.

Another Amazon monopoly-building behavior might be easier to handle legally, though Nina's lawsuit doesn't mention this one either: the fact that Amazon is a platform and competitor at the same time. Amazon Marketplace, which represents billions of dollars in revenue and a majority of Amazon's retail sales, works like this: Amazon lets small businesses sell things on their Amazon Marketplace website in exchange for some fees, which now can exceed a frankly obscene 50% of each purchase.[59] That's a problem, and here's another: Amazon also sells their own products on Amazon Marketplace, giving them key advantages. Free advertising, for one. For another, a trove of product data that they use (read: steal) to make their own competing products. This is fundamentally unfair, and it has allowed Amazon to basically take over the entire ecommerce market. Making it illegal to both host and sell on a platform would be a major step towards protecting bookstores and other small businesses. A bill to do just that, the American Innovation and Choice Online Act, started to move through Congress in 2021, but failed to receive a full vote in either the House or the Senate. As of 2023, with a Republican-controlled House, its prospects are uncertain.

You may be asking, aren't monopolies illegal? Isn't the government supposed to intervene to prevent anticompetitive behavior in free markets? Yes. But here's the problem: for the last four decades, the enforcement of antitrust law has been totally kneecapped in favor of letting big companies get as big as they want. In the 1970s and 1980s, while France was passing its bookstore-protecting Lang Law, far-right economist and judge Robert Bork introduced a radical new interpretation of American antitrust law. Rather than encouraging competition, in Bork's thinking, antitrust law should focus on what he called "consumer welfare." In plain language, that means regulators shouldn't worry about how big companies are, as long as the companies keep prices low. This thinking was embraced by the influential Chicago School of Economics and, ultimately, Ronald Reagan.

And so we find ourselves at the tail end of four decades of flaccid antitrust enforcement. It's a tale of two governments: as we've already observed in a previous chapter, French bookstores have largely flourished since the 1980s. In America, meanwhile, if a company can prove they're lowering prices, they're free to get as big as they want and there's nothing regulators can do. Hence, it's hard to stop Amazon from being so big and anticompetitive because Amazon generally has low prices on retail goods. Even if a Lang Law clone never happens in the United States, a good policy switch to protect bookstores is simply to return to a more pro-competitive theory of antitrust law, where a company's holistic competitive effects are the basis for antitrust enforcement.

Fortunately, there's some exciting movement in this regard. The Biden administration has been sympathetic to those calling for antitrust reform, as reflected most clearly in a few appointments of key neo-antitrust folks like FTC chair Lina Khan and DOJ Antitrust Division head Jonathan Kanter. This reinvigorated antitrust movement faced its first major test in trying to block the merger of mega-publishers Penguin Random House and Simon & Schuster. Notably, the DOJ's case focused on the deal's hindering competition, not its pricing effects. The DOJ won handily, with Judge Florence Pan eviscerating the publishers' case in a blistering opinion that claimed that "the effect of [the proposed merger] may be substantially to lessen competition."[60] This is a big deal, and it may represent a turning point in antitrust enforcement. In a statement, Institute for Local Self-Reliance co-director Stacy Mitchell said the ruling represented "the beginning of the end of the consumer welfare standard, which has warped and enfeebled antitrust enforcement for the last 40 years."[61] After the decision came down, *Vulture* blogger Victoria Bekiempis called out what many in the book industry were also thinking: that Amazon surely must be next. She writes, "The elephant in the room throughout all of this continues to be Amazon, as the Big Five still seemingly feel like

David to Amazon's Goliath. With this merger now blocked, Amazon continues to write everyone's rules."[62] A clear way to protect bookstores, then, is to keep pushing to reinvigorate the antitrust movement so that it can successfully take on this corporate giant.

Ultimately, Amazon is a systemic problem that can only be fully addressed through systemic solutions (like antitrust enforcement). Still, though, there are small steps that individual readers can take to resist Amazon in their own lives. One is to stop reviewing books on Goodreads. Consider this: Goodreads is owned by Amazon. Goodreads is also a deeply flawed platform with little to no safeguards against spamming negative reviews, which can and does lead to coordinated attacks against authors. Despite this, Amazon has begun including Goodreads reviews on Amazon book product pages. The idea is simple: Above all else, Amazon is a data company obsessed with gobbling up as much data about consumers as it possibly can. So when you rate a book on Goodreads, you're telling Amazon valuable info about your reading habits. Readers handing over free data to Amazon makes it easier for Amazon to sell books to readers, and the more books Amazon sells, the more of a grip it has on the US book market. Fortunately, there are bookstore-friendly alternatives for those seeking an online reader network. I personally like the StoryGraph. But which platform you migrate to isn't as important as divesting from Amazon. (And let us not forget that it can be much more rewarding and pleasant to share data about your reading life via conversation, perhaps with a book club or a bookseller.)

Another common reading tool owned by enemy-of-bookstores Amazon is Audible. As the owner of Audible, Amazon has a huge stranglehold on the audiobook market. Through predatory consumer practices, as well as restrictive technology called digital rights management, Audible has claimed a gigantic share of the market, by some estimations upwards of 90%.[63] There's good news, though: Libro.fm, a startup audiobook platform, has the same functionality and much of the same inventory as Audible. You subscribe, you get monthly credits, you use a mobile app. Only in Libro's case, a portion of your purchase goes to bookstores instead of to Jeff Bezos. You can even pick which bookstore gets the percentage of your sale. Helping bookstores stake a claim, no matter how small, in the Amazon-dominated audiobook market will help protect them.

Unfortunately, when it comes to the ebook market, Amazon's grip is even stronger, and there isn't a one-size-fits-all alternative. According to Rebecca Giblin and Cory Doctorow's book *Chokepoint Capitalism*, Amazon has built an "enduring chokepoint" of the ebook market, capturing "fully 90 percent" of ebook sales in the first two years of the Kindle's existence and refusing to let up since.[64] For all intents and purposes, Amazon remains the only way to read ebooks. This was a calculated objective that Amazon spent years working towards: early on, Jeff Bezos told an executive working on the Kindle project to "proceed as if your goal is to put everyone selling physical books out of a job."[65] Basically, Amazon ebooks have super restrictive digital rights management (DRM) that only lets them be viewed on Amazon devices or apps. Further, because of DRM, you never actually buy an ebook from Amazon. Rather, you essentially lease the right to access it. Amazon sells this access, as well as the devices needed to use it, at predatorily low prices. To achieve these low prices, Amazon bullies publishers into contracts that allow this monopolizing long game to happen.

At one point, much too late, four major US publishers got together to fight back against Amazon's unfair ebook practices. In response, US antitrust enforcers punished *the publishers* for anticompetitive behavior. This as Amazon established near-total control over the ebook sector. As Giblin and Doctorow put it, "The publishers were affronted. How could *they* be liable for anticompetitive conduct when they only did what they did to counteract Amazon's own bullying?

But that's how it currently works."[66] Ironically, if the four publishers had merged into one monopolizing mega-company, they could have proceeded with their ebook action. Regardless, now that Amazon has captured nearly all of the ebook market, it's really hard to convince people to switch. They've spent years building libraries that aren't compatible with any other platforms. Because Amazon isn't removing their DRM anytime soon, users would have to start over fresh if they switched. Giblin and Doctorow call this a "cost moat," and it's a key advantage tech monopolies use to stay in power: switching to a non-monopolizing, bookstore-friendly alternative would just be too expensive.

However, there is some reason for hope: as of this writing, Bookshop.org has announced an ebook pilot program set to launch in 2023 or 2024 in the United States. To really protect bookstores, it's essential that we support these efforts to build bookstore-friendly ebook platforms that will attract users and loosen Amazon's chokehold on the market.

## ACTION STEP: MONEY FOR BOOKSTORES IN CRISIS

It's hard to imagine Bookends & Beginnings finding a way to continue operating in the wake of their oppressive rent increase without the $100,000+ they raised on GoFundMe. I've already established that bookstores are a low-margin business, and that this fact often leads to too-low wages. It also means that very few bookstores have any significant rainy-day money, especially bookstores like Bookends & Beginnings who make a point to try to fairly compensate their employees. We also have seen, thanks to folks like Avid Bookshop, that small-business-focused financing isn't as accessible as it should be. That all means that when an emergency happens, bookstores often have to turn to their communities to raise money to deal with it. Many bookstores have been saved by overwhelmingly positive responses to crowdfunding campaigns, especially at the uncertain and frightening beginning of the Covid pandemic. This is a really straightforward and direct way to protect bookstores, for those who have the means: when bookstores ask for money online, give it to them. Small donations coming together to raise a six-figure sum to save a bookstore is a perfect example of how individual choices together in community can create something bigger. Keep an eye out (bookstores usually announce fundraising efforts via newsletter and social media) and donate when you can.

# CHAPTER 7:
# "CAN'T REVOLUTIONIZE FROM A U-HAUL TRUCK"

## Semicolon Bookstore & Gallery, Chicago, IL

F or Danni Mullen, owner of Chicago's Semicolon Bookstore & Gallery, the first indication that anything was going on was the flood of order notification emails pouring into her inbox while she was on vacation. Thousands and thousands of them in the first hour alone. The sudden onset of all these orders gave her a bad feeling. She tells me, "I was like, 'I'm sorry. What just happened?' And then I watched the news, and I thought, 'Oh no. Oh no.'" George Floyd had been murdered by police in Minneapolis, and the country erupted in protest.

I'm stunned when she tells me this. The first she heard of George Floyd's murder was the flood of orders her store received? She explains, to my mounting horror: "I saw the orders first. Because when I go on vacation, I don't check the news. I do check my email from the store, just in case there's something important. I saw the orders first. Then I saw the news and I'm like, 'This can't be why we're getting orders.' And I'll be damned if it was."

That summer, in the wake of Floyd's murder, Black-owned bookstores like Semicolon bore the brunt of white readers' renewed attempts to understand racism in America. For countless people, that meant ordering certain nonfiction titles like Ibram X. Kendi's *How to Be an Antiracist* from Black-owned bookstores, who crumbled under the weight. Danni claims that Semicolon had a staggering $2 million in orders in the first 24 hours. While that much business might seem like good news, it came dangerously close to completely overwhelming the business. Danni says, "Once I found out what happened, I knew that surge of white guilt was going to shut us down. We had a team of four. There was no way we were going to fulfill all these orders." But they had no choice. Danni immediately flew from LA back to Chicago. Once she was back, she and her team did 18-hour shifts every day, fulfilling $150,000 worth of orders a day to try to dig out from under the mountain of demand.

There was some good news in the deluge: the increased business allowed Semicolon to open to foot traffic one day a week, their first in-person business since shutting down because of Covid in March 2020. Danni was also able to provide cars for booksellers who didn't have them, making it easier for them to get to work to help with the torrent of orders. But ultimately, I don't think Danni and her team would want to do it again. The impulse to buy an Ibram X. Kendi book and post about it on social media to absolve white guilt felt performative to Danni, who says, "That time sucked because you get all these orders, but then you get all these people who place the orders and never even pick them up. They never picked them up. They didn't want these books. They just wanted to post the little stupid thing on Instagram." Danni doesn't even think books like Robin DiAngelo's *White Fragility* are where white people should turn to sort through whatever guilt or confusion they're feeling. When discussing the widely shared reading lists that proliferated in the days after George Floyd's murder, Danni emphatically tells me, "Do not send people these wack-ass lists. These are not the books you should be reading if you want to be anti-racist. If you want to be anti-racist, you have to build empathy. You should read fiction for that." All of the pressures combined proved to be too much, and the influx of business and attention was nearly the end of the Semicolon story. She explains, "Every snide-ass newspaper article that came out about Black booksellers and our inability to keep up was really, really harmful to our psyche. We constantly had to fight and defend, which is true every day, but it was amped up a hundred times during that moment."

Of course, Black booksellers shouldn't have *had* to keep up. To place this much burden on Black-owned businesses during an already-traumatic time is unfair. If white people's self-education about racism is traumatizing Black people, it's doing the opposite of what it should. No matter the intention, placing unreasonable expectations on Black-owned businesses during a time of racial trauma is a form of racism. Danni explains, "When you bring all those orders in and people are like, 'Will my order be here tomorrow if I order today?' Absolutely the fuck not. Those conversations are microaggressions in themselves." Listening to Danni talk about it, I see that there's lingering pain, even years later: "It was bad. My entire team came to me and said it was too much and they loved the store, but they never expected it to feel that way. I had an entire team quit on me at one time. And I got it. I wanted to quit too. My name just happens to be on the lease."

Speaking of leases, summer 2020's chaos wasn't the last time Semicolon's story came dangerously close to a premature end. Danni and I are talking in Semicolon's spacious new location on Milwaukee Avenue in Chicago's Wicker Park neighborhood, a bustling area with pedestrians and trendy restaurants and shops. We're on leather couches in a huge back room, with Danni's five-month-old German Shepherd contentedly snoozing between us. The back end of Semicolon is a maze of storage rooms and workspaces, including a small screen-printing machine where they make their own merch. The front of the store is a riot of colors, with murals by local artists and framed illustrations exploding all over the walls as '90s hip-hop booms from hidden speakers. A team of cheerful booksellers is preparing books for off-site events—Semicolon has several today alone—as a few customers pop in and out. These spacious digs, while luxurious, are something of an accident.

Danni came to the bookselling industry via a circuitous path, after personal tragedy. In January 2019, Danni was diagnosed with ocular melanoma and her recovery forced her to stop working for the first time since she was 15. "I had to kind of sit still for a second," she tells me. "I never knew how to do that." Clearly a person with too much energy to be content doing nothing, Danni "went into a really deep depression." When her wife told her doing something, anything, would help, Danni took to the streets. "I would go for these long walks all over the city because I'd never explored Chicago," she explains. On one such walk through the West Town neighborhood, she passed a building with a "for lease" sign. Without thinking much about it, she called the landlord. The landlord, desperate to have the space occupied, offered to rent it for $1,500 a month, far below market rate for such a space in Chicago. "Twelve hours later, I have a lease," Danni says, "but I have zero plans. My wife is pissed. She was like, 'We don't have any money. How are we going to do this?' And I decide that I want to be surrounded by the things I love the most. Chemo sucks. Everything sucks at that moment. Put me with the books and the art." And so Semicolon, a space for books and art, was born. They hand-built the shelves. They called in favors from their artist friends to paint the walls. They bought books from Goodwill initially, until they learned more about the publishing industry, enough to set up publisher accounts. They studied other bookstores, they looked for tips online, they built a team. They tried to figure out the secret to bookstore longevity.

Here's one part of that secret: amicable landlords willing to charge below market rate. Semicolon had that, until they didn't. Danni tells me, "We got to the store one day, and the door was padlocked. Our landlord got foreclosed on. Did not tell us." Until that point, Semicolon was finding their footing after a rocky, essentially accidental start. They were building a community. Some of their social media stuff was going viral. They were finding a voice. At some points they had lines out the door. Then, all of a sudden, their entire business was behind a lock they didn't have the key to. They called their attorney. The attorney called the landlord's bank. The bank said they'd remove the padlocks for 30 days. Danni and team could operate the store for those 30 days, but they also had to find another space in that time frame. This is a huge challenge anywhere, but it's even worse in one of the country's hottest commercial real estate markets. Danni sums up her feelings on the challenge when she tells me, "It was a sucky time."

Despite the heat in Chicago's commercial renting marketplace, Danni found Semicolon's new space on the first day of looking. It was in a busy neighborhood. It was in great shape. It was huge, four times the size of the original Semicolon. The only problem? The rent at this spot was ten times as much as the old space. But Danni felt like she didn't have a choice. Her old landlord's bank was only giving her a month to move out. So she went about signing the expensive and huge new space. How did the new landlord trust that Danni and Semicolon could handle the huge increase in rent? Eventually, he told Danni the only reason he offered her a lease is that Semicolon was verified on Instagram.

So, in October 2021, Semicolon moved in, hauling everything five minutes up the street into the new Wicker Park location. When I ask her about that time, Danni repeats a theme, saying that "everything sucked." One reason for that: moving costs, deposits, lease expenses, and everything else totaled about $300,000. Another reason: on the new location's opening day, Danni got a call from the old landlord's bank. After reconsidering Danni's situation, the bank offered to extend

Semicolon's original lease on their old space to five years. Turns out, Semicolon didn't have to move to their expensive new spot after all. But, alas, they already had. Ultimately, Danni decided to hang on to the cheap lease on the old space and use it for events and storage, hoping to make things work out at the new location. She had already signed. What other choice did she have but to at least attempt to function in the big new space?

So Semicolon settled into their colorful new spot, which though expensive, was wonderful. I can attest to that: it has giant glass doors, tons of natural light, high ceilings, and a spacious sales floor peppered with energetic booksellers. It's a good feeling. Danni knows that feeling is one of her strengths: "I believe in vibes. If people come in and they love it, then they're going to tell everybody. And so, we make sure when we have people in the store, our team is having a good time. We speak to everybody who walks in. We become best friends with everybody who walks in and we have an 83% return rate on customers." But it's not all smooth sailing. That rent hike is a persistent issue. Danni admits, "I have been carrying Semicolon since February, financially. Just carrying us, just getting us to the next moment where we can make some excess." When I ask her what would've happened if the store were owned by someone unable to prop it up with their personal finances, Danni says, simply, that "the store would be closed."

Despite all this, Semicolon seems like it's having the most fun. In addition to the vibrant, energetic, literally colorful in-store experience, Danni has found huge audiences online through social media and through tons of traditional media, like a TV appearance on *Ellen*. I ask her about her knack for going viral, and Semicolon's engaging social media strategy. I tell her it seems pretty savvy from my perspective. Danni corrects me: "It seems savvy, but it's a method of protection." She continues:

I don't want to continue going through a hundred "I hate n****s" emails every day. That's harmful. But if we're loud enough and if enough people see us, then we become something that's above harming. And that's the only way I think we can get there. And we do a good job of that on social media. It's peacocking. That's what we do. If you see me, you cannot attack me.

As the weight of this sentiment sinks in for me, I ask Danni what she wants for her bookstore, and for Black-owned bookstores in general. At first she talks about building ownership, saying (understandably, given her experience), "Landlords are shitty. They're shitty all around. There's no good landlord because that's not what they're in it for. Landlords aren't landlords to help you out. They're landlords so that they can make a lot of money off of you and ideally your business." Danni wishes for it to be easier for her bookstore and other Black-owned bookstores to own their buildings, since "it's a big thing that you don't have to worry about." She adds, "That's what bookstores were meant to be, a community hub, a hub for revolution. And we can't revolutionize when we're moving. Can't revolutionize from a U-Haul truck."

But Danni adds one more thing that she wants for her bookstore and for all Black-owned bookstores. She's as emphatic as she's been this whole time, which is saying something. What she wants, ultimately, is basic, and something that a lot of booksellers take for granted:

My dream for the future of Black-owned bookstores is just to feel comfortable. I don't know if other booksellers know or even have time to think about how much discomfort we carry on a regular basis. But the fact is, I have to constantly watch my cameras to see who is throwing things, running, or who is shooting at our store today. And that is every Black bookseller. I would like to have the same comfort as every other bookseller.

·  ·  ·

I talked to Danni at Semicolon on August 10, 2022, and wrote the preceding profile the following week. In December 2022, Danni took a major step towards the comfort and security she craves for herself and other Black bookstores: she returned to Semicolon's original River West building, moving out of the expensive new Wicker Park location. More importantly, she started working on an offer to buy Semicolon's original building. No more landlords for Semicolon, at least for the time being. Though the Wicker Park location was gorgeous and vast, constant plumbing issues and other maintenance problems caused surprise closures and headaches for the Semicolon team. In discussions with the Wicker Park landlord, Danni was able to leverage these issues to get out of that staggeringly expensive lease early, freeing her up to make an offer on the original building. Since Danni had been keeping up with the original building's cheap lease all along, using it as storage space, she was able to quickly move Semicolon back to its original spot. In the original space, Danni is looking to take on projects like making the entrance wheelchair accessible, renting out the building's apartments, and converting the basement to retail space. But ultimately, she's just glad to have a spot that's hers where she can build a lasting Semicolon legacy. An article about the move in *Block Club Chicago* quotes Danni as saying, simply, "Permanence is necessary."[67]

·  ·  ·

Both Semicolon and Bookends & Beginnings have a lot in common: both are Chicago-area stores with outspoken owners who are dedicated to their communities, and both faced landlord crises that almost meant the end of their businesses. The fact that this book outlines two landlord crises with two happy (for now) endings does not mean that all bad-landlord stories end this way. Who knows how many small businesses have faced an unsustainable rent increase and simply decided to close up shop. A rent increase like the one Nina faced can turn a business from thriving to imperiled instantly. Similarly, there are many who, unlike Danni, wouldn't have the means or opportunity to purchase a building from their former landlord. Something needs to change about commercial renting; high commercial rents are a threat to bookstores, yes, but also to the urban fabric of America.

# ACTION STEP: BETTER LANDLORDS

The fact of sky-high commercial rents is putting a strain on many, if not most, bookstores. None of the action steps in this book are silver bullets, but I guarantee that if you could press a button that instantly halved the rent for every bookstore in the country, it would be a game changer for the future of bookstores in America.

I'll try to be charitable about this and imagine a reason for the rent crisis other than simple greed. I suppose there could be lots of explanations. If you ask a landlord, they'll probably blame city policy or property tax payments or building maintenance costs. Granted, I suppose it is possible that some terrible landlords are not being terrible on purpose—that property taxes and other city policies are indeed forcing them to charge exorbitant rates to small-business tenants. If that's the case, though, small businesses should not bear the costs. Rather, those city policies need to change. This isn't a debate; as Nina put it, it's "a battle for the soul of Evanston" and countless other cities. Landlord issues range from "pain in the ass" (maintenance issues, building condition, rents that are too high) to existential (being forced to move because of rent or other factors). Across the country, exorbitant commercial rents are threatening the fabric of urban life. This book makes the case that small businesses, especially bookstores, provide countless economic and cultural benefits to their communities. A landlord who is also a good local citizen, then, will find it in their interest to make it possible for a bookstore to operate in their space. For the first 30 years of the Raven's history, we had a landlord who charged well below market rate on rent simply because he thought it was good for a bookstore to be in that building. Why aren't there more landlords like this, who view the existence of a bookstore as the community investment it actually is? Under no circumstances should it make sense for a landlord to keep a storefront empty. Under no circumstances should a bookstore have to shut down because it can't pay its impossibly high rent. Whatever needs to change to end that, it needs to change now.

## ACTION STEP: BETTER ONLINE CITIZENSHIP

Semicolon's flood of online orders in the wake of George Floyd's murder didn't end up being the blessing that many thought it would. Yes, it meant more business, but it also meant white people overwhelming a Black business in an attempt to absolve their guilt. On top of all that, during that summer, Semicolon and many other bookstores buckled under the weight of impossible expectations. Amazon has worked really hard to create the impression that books should be shipped fast and for "free" (though of course, Prime subscriptions aren't free). This has created a widespread expectation that a book should arrive at your door 24–48 hours after you click "buy." The only reason Amazon can fulfill this expectation is that they're willing to create dangerous and grueling warehouse and delivery conditions. For everyone else, it's an impossible task, especially when huge demand has sent certain books to reprints. That all leads to email inboxes filled with demanding, aggressive, or even hateful customers. For Semicolon, this was on top of the everyday barrage of hate and harassment they face just from being a Black bookstore in the 21st century. This online negativity has a strong emotional impact; it's not a matter of just deleting and forgetting about it. To protect bookstores and offset this online negativity, look for positive ways to support them online.

One way to do just that is to write a positive review. The Raven is fortunate enough to have a pretty good set of online reviews, and we're grateful for the positive ones. We're less grateful for the one-star reviews, many of which are unfair or nonsensical. (One called us a "woke joke"; another called me conceited. Still another claimed we were "mask nazis," which is a real fun thing for a Jewish bookseller to be called.) Still, there are those who do use a store's proximity to five stars as a metric when weighing whether or not to support it. Plus, "review bombing" is a tool used by far-right crusaders when they target a business; they'll organize a campaign to post numerous one-star reviews of the business, despite never having set foot there. Aside from trying to report all the negative reviews, the only way to combat this is to ask your actual customers to write positive ones. In the end, despite the flaws of the five-star industrial complex, a good online review is another fast and free way to protect a bookstore.

# CHAPTER 8:
# "I CAN'T PRETEND WE'RE NEUTRAL ANYMORE"

## Moon Palace Books, Minneapolis, MN

So many images from Minneapolis in the summer of 2020 still stick in my mind. Of course, the horrific video of George Floyd's senseless murder, which so many people will never be able to forget. Even if people wanted to avoid the video, it was everywhere. So were the images of the aftermath. I remember sitting in my apartment, hundreds of miles away, watching the Unicorn Riot streams. I remember the first flames coming from the windows of the Third Precinct. I remember the building, engulfed. The mysterious figure lurking by the AutoZone. So many people in the street feeling so much pain. I also remember a photograph of Moon Palace Books. It showed Moon Palace's huge rainbow building, a few doors down from the smoldering Third Precinct. Even in peaceful times the building has a way of towering over the neighborhood. But on those nights of pain, Moon Palace rose not over neighbors but over ruins. The neighborhood was in flames. The bookstore was untouched. Its windows were covered in plywood. The plywood was covered with six-foot-tall letters that said, "Abolish the police." I remember that photo.

· · ·

Two years later, I drive to Minneapolis to hear Moon Palace co-owner Angela Schwesnedl tell me the story of those nights. I know parts of the story. A few months after the protests in

2020, I had the honor of presenting Angela and her husband and fellow co-owner, Jamie, with the Midwest Independent Booksellers Association's Bookseller of the Year Award. In my speech, I spoke about those nights of pain and protest. Here's how I told the story as I understood it:

> Angela and Jamie fed protestors free pizza from the store's restaurant, Geek Love Café. When protestors offered to pay, Jamie told them to donate to George Floyd's family. When the police tried to set up a staging area in Moon Palace's parking lot, Jamie forced them away. Some folks believed these actions of solidarity are what led Moon Palace to be spared damage in the protests, but Jamie and Angela weren't acting to save their business or their building or their books. They were acting for justice. Jamie even told people not to risk themselves protecting the store. He was quoted in the New York Times saying, "Things that may be lost or damaged in our building are just things, but your life is priceless, just like George Floyd's life was priceless. Be safe."

> Watching this unfold from afar made me believe that a bookstore owner does not in fact need to feel helpless, that a bookstore can and should figure out a way to do something. Moon Palace acted—and is acting—how a bookstore should act in turbulent times. This is how a bookstore can be an engine for positive social change. This is how a bookstore can protect and serve its neighborhood.

In the years since the George Floyd protests, and since I presented Moon Palace with the MIBA award, I've realized that the store's work is even more important and inspiring than giving protestors pizza and blocking their parking lot from the cops. As galvanizing as those actions may be, Moon Palace does much more every day. One thing I did get 100% right: Moon Palace is a bookstore determined to protect and serve its neighborhood, in times of peace and in times of pain.

•   •   •

In late spring of 2022, Moon Palace still towers over its stretch of Minnehaha Avenue in South Minneapolis. Across the street, what was the 27th Avenue Post Office is a grassy field encased in leaning chain link. Up the road a little ways is an AutoZone I remember from watching videos—people yelling at a shadowy figure in a gas mask who sure looked like an arsonist trying to sabotage the protests. And just a few hundred feet north of Moon Palace stands the Third Precinct, untouched since May 28, 2020, the night it burned. Jersey barriers, barbed wire, and concrete blocks form a rickety fortress around the charred brick and plywood. Weeds sprout among the concrete. Waterlogged protest signs litter the ground. It's as if the world has pushed pause on the building and forgotten about it for two years. But people have not forgotten, especially the people of South Minneapolis.

In stark contrast to the Third Precinct, Moon Palace is once again vibrant. It's full of customers and books, its colorful exterior a beacon for the book lovers of South Minneapolis. Its windows have shed their defiant plywood, opting instead for show flyers and a view of the store's cavernous and modern interior. Upstairs, the window that bore the "Police" part of "Abolish the Police" now shows leaning stacks of boxes, evidence of pandemic years spent bookselling online.

After a quick and pleasant browse, of course, I try to find Angela. Turns out, she's camped out in the darkened booths of Geek Love Café, Moon Palace's pizza restaurant left long dormant thanks to the pandemic. The store has been rearranged, so I have to slide aside a bookcase to get to Angela, or even know the restaurant is there. It's a fitting setting for a chat with one of the most soft-spoken booksellers I know. Colorful Moon Palace has made headlines; they've spraypainted six-foot abolitionist slogans on the outside of their rainbow building, but you get the feeling that Angela might prefer to do her work this way: camped out in some quiet corner of the bookstore, difficult to even find.

Very quickly, our conversation turns to May 2020. She remembers being on the phone with a Penguin Random House credit rep when she said, "I'm sorry, I'm going to have to go. They're teargassing again." She remembers thinking, "I can't pretend we're neutral anymore." She remembers a message from her mom showing a picture of the store in the *New York Times*. She describes the photo to me, saying, "It looked like the National Guard and the police were protecting the store instead of really harassing my customers and teargassing people." As soon as Angela saw the picture, and its incorrect implied meaning, she and Jamie rallied their community to paint "Abolish the Police" on the plywood covering Moon Palace's windows. That way, Angela says, "the next time the media tried to put us in the news," there would be no doubt about where Moon Palace stood on police violence and who makes the neighborhood safe. Spoiler alert: it's not the police. "I was so pissed off," Angela says. Though it was born out of Angela and Jamie's anger at being misperceived in the paper of record, the sign was a community effort—neighborhood folks helping a neighborhood store: "People in the neighborhood came, they took care of that for me. I think it was 4 a.m., 5 a.m. I couldn't sleep."

This is the stuff I didn't see on CNN. But it's the stuff Angela, Jamie, and Moon Palace remember the most. Angela recalls, "The whole neighborhood took care of not only me and not only the store, but everybody. There were just people feeding people, the food lines were blocks long because nobody could get food and nobody could get anything they needed."

The memory of one offer of help still stands out to Angela: the very same day Angela had to hang up on the Penguin Random House credit rep because the cops were teargassing outside the store, she got another call. A calm, reassuring, elegant voice was on the other line. In all the chaos, it took Angela a minute to realize who it was and what they were saying. It was Louise Erdrich. She was offering to pick up Moon Palace's outgoing mail because she knew the post office across the street had burned down. Angela pulled it together enough to tell Louise thanks, but it probably wasn't worth it to drive down to Moon Palace on a day when the neighborhood was literally smoldering. While the Louise Erdrich mail run never materialized, Angela clearly relishes telling the story to this day. But it's more than just a famous author and fellow bookseller calling to offer help. The community coming together to heal and support itself in the wake of the protests and the police's exit inspired Moon Palace. Angela explains, "I think that really changed where I saw us positioned: 'Oh this is it. We're really here.'" It was not the crisis but the community-driven mutual aid response that galvanized Moon Palace and solidified their role as activists, abolitionists, and neighbors. Angela explains, "We were always the nice liberal bookstore." In the new world, in a neighborhood reshaped by violence, "nice liberal" wouldn't cut it anymore.

I'm realizing I've gotten this far without really talking about Moon Palace as a bookstore. Their community work is vital, and they're heroes of mine for political reasons (as is probably apparent by this point). But I'd be remiss if I didn't say Moon Palace is also a really, really good place to browse for books. It's a force for good in its neighborhood, but it's also a great bookstore. That's the important part, I think. To do both. Moon Palace is a roomy, modern, bright store with sky-high ceilings and simple light-wood bookcases arranged in an unpredictable maze. To my delight, a giant poetry section hulks right inside the front door. Aside from the clean, welcoming feel of the room, the layout itself is full of surprises. As I was browsing fiction—a section absolutely stuffed with small-press translated titles—I turned around and found myself looking at business books. The music section is right by sci-fi. It's not so much that the store's layout is haphazard, like some dusty used-book warren. Rather, it's purposefully unpredictable. When I ask her about her store's oddball layout, Angela says, simply, "I love chaos." She continues, "If it were only me in the store working, it would just be chaos, random books on the shelves everywhere for that ultimate discovery." Shelfmaking taken to its eccentric extreme. It's an interesting idea—at the Raven, one of our most persistent staff debates is how to label sections and where to put them. Moon Palace has taken a different approach, with the thought that smashing together romance and poetry may, through proximity, lead the poetry reader to discover a romance or vice versa. Taken together, the whole philosophy is a bit more open-minded than other stores known for abolitionist politics. Angela says, "I always wanted to be the kind of store that sold a wide variety of stuff. I felt like people who read poetry also read romance and also read books about abolition." Not to belabor the point, but one of the most important things about Moon Palace, in my mind, is that it's an abolitionist force in its neighborhood *and* it's a bookstore that caters to all kinds of neighborhood readers. Sometimes those goals overlap, sometimes they don't, but it doesn't seem like Moon Palace is planning on pulling back from either front anytime soon.

Still, much about the future remains uncertain. For one thing, when I visited Moon Palace in spring 2022, the police had unofficially started talking about moving back into the Third Precinct—as this book goes to print, there still aren't many details. According to Angela, the police aren't being very transparent with the neighborhood regarding the future of the Third Precinct building, and that makes some area folks uneasy. She says, "The city's been super vague about what's happening, what the process is, deciding what happens to the building or the space. All that's strategic. The more obscured the decision-making process, the harder it is for something to happen." Whereas some businesses in the area cheer a potential return of the police and the subsequent reduction in response times, Angela remains committed to abolitionist community care. She tells me, "I don't want them to kill someone in the name of the store. I don't want them to kill someone for me. . . . There's no police response time that makes that worth it."

Moon Palace's transformation from "nice liberals" into abolitionist leaders has solidified Angela's feelings about a potential return of the police to her corner of South Minneapolis: "I don't want them back on my block. We don't want the police precinct back. Not everybody really feels comfortable saying that publicly. I'm okay saying that publicly because there's no hiding now. Everybody knows how I feel." One of the reasons why everybody knows how she feels is that she's not afraid to say it, and she feels obligated to say it as much as possible. She explains, "Since [George Floyd's] murder I've gone to every small-business meeting I can. The rhetoric [the police] use is that they're protecting small businesses and that we want them here. So no matter how busy I am, I'm going to show up at those meetings so that nobody can say, 'Well, we *all* want more police.'" It's one thing Angela can do, and she does it all the time. She's soft-spoken and unassuming, but she thinks the community is less safe with more police, and her presence in any given Zoom screen or conference room is a guarantee that the abolitionists won't be silenced. She says, "I'm not very intimidating, but my presence can be there. I can show up and do that."

•　　•　　•

In a really clear way, Moon Palace Books demonstrates the tight bonds between a bookstore and its community. The community that Moon Palace serves—the readers of South Minneapolis—was forced into crisis by George Floyd's murder. Moon Palace responded immediately, and has never stopped responding. They fed protestors and defended their parking lot from the police, and now, years later, they're still dealing with the fallout by remaining engaged in abolitionist organizing and local politics. The whole story demonstrates two vital components of working to create a more just community: the importance of local media, and the importance of showing up for local politics.

## ACTION STEP: READ AND SUPPORT LOCAL NEWS

To start our discussion of local news and local bookstores, let's consider police violence and media coverage, a question deeply relevant to the story of Moon Palace Books over the last few years. Corporate media has repeatedly shown a pro-police, anti-protestor bias in its reporting of incidents like George Floyd's murder. Writing for Salon.com, Robin Anderson claims that "legacy and corporate media portrayed BLM demonstrators across the United States as violent and chaotic, despite subsequent evidence that, in 97 percent of cases, protests were peaceful and nonviolent."[68] Additionally, mainstream media has a habit of parroting artificially neutral language from police press releases, often employing phrases like "officer-involved shooting" to linguistically strip accountability from police actions.[69] Indeed, imagine what media coverage of George Floyd's murder would have looked like had Darnella Frazier not filmed the violent officers. What would the story have been if the police had been able to give the first and last word about what happened, with no public evidence to the contrary? A fast-consolidating corporate media landscape, with fewer news sources all controlled by larger corporations, will lead to a higher likelihood that news coverage of police violence will simply repeat police talking points. This will silence voices like Angela Schwesnedl, voices focused on mutual aid and the neighborhood's actual, hyper-local needs. A proliferation of locally owned, independent media sources will increase the likelihood that voices like Angela's can be amplified. Bookstores doing neighborhood-focused community work will find this work easier in a media landscape filled with independent, local coverage.

But local newspapers are in crisis. Here's a concise version of what happened: Craigslist killed newspaper classifieds, eliminating a crucial revenue source for local papers. Then the advertising arms of Amazon, Google, and Facebook killed newspaper ads altogether, eating up the ad money that used to pay for journalist salaries. Thus hobbled, local newspapers across the country found themselves in dire financial straits. This left them ripe for purchase by massive corporations, a few of which (like Gannett or Ogden) began gobbling up local papers. Even worse, according to Cory Doctorow and Rebecca Giblin, "Many of these papers were purchased using a sketchy financial maneuver called a leveraged buyout; this saddles a paper with debt and commonly leads its new owners to adopt cost-saving measures like firing journalists and cutting arts coverage."[70]

To further illustrate the urgency of varied and independent local news coverage, we can also return to the story of the attack on the St. Marys library, as told in Chapter 2. My main source for this story was coverage written by Rachel Mipro for the *Kansas Reflector*. The *Reflector* is an independent nonprofit news organization reporting on Kansas government issues, founded in the wake of the *Topeka Capital-Journal*'s 2017 sale to a newspaper-gobbling mega-corporation. The St. Marys article came to my attention because it was republished in another hyper-local nonprofit news publication, the *Lawrence Times*. The *LT* was founded by Mackenzie Clark, a former reporter for the *Lawrence Journal-World*, the legacy newspaper in the Raven's hometown of Lawrence, Kansas. Guess what? In 2016, the *Journal-World* was bought by Ogden, who then proceeded to empty its printing plant and impose dramatic cuts to staff.

It's interesting to note that the first, best, most thorough coverage of the St. Marys library attack came from the *Kansas Reflector* and the *Lawrence Times*, not the area's two monopoly-owned traditional newspapers. Without the dogged work of two small, independent news organizations, how much would this story be covered in Kansas at all? There are real-life consequences to this: the city commissioners themselves said public outcry is what kept the library alive; what kind of outcry can be mustered if the public doesn't know about the issue in the first place? So it's easy to imagine the story escaping notice, period, further silencing any queer or pro-free-speech voices in St. Marys.

But providing accurate, independent coverage of community issues isn't the only way that local newspapers benefit bookstores. For one thing, newspapers help drive event attendance and book sales when they report on certain books or authors; the targeted, literary, hyper-local audience of a paper is one of the best advertising markets you could ask for. For another, local newspapers often run annual "best of the city" competitions, which can lead to increased traffic for a bookstore. Of course, these contests are a way to sell ads to the businesses featured in the thousands of categories. But ad grabs aside, the readership on this stuff is pretty high, and some people do find the Raven because we regularly win "best bookstore in Lawrence." Voting for your bookstore, then, is one fast and free way to protect it.

The bottom line is that a bookstore thrives best in a healthy community filled with engaged citizens, and it's hard to maintain that kind of community without a functioning local newspaper. As the story of corporate media takeover and upstart local news outlets plays out across the country, there are a few ways you can help. It's one thing to subscribe to a newspaper limping along under the weight of a bad leveraged buyout and a distant corporate owner. But another crucial part of the work is supporting the people blazing a path towards what's next. Find the people writing the good stuff about your communities and read their work. Even better, pay for it (the Raven is a proud and longtime sponsor of the *Lawrence Times*, and I've contributed a few op-eds to the *Reflector*). It'll uplift your entire community, and the benefits will reach your bookstore and everyone else.

# ACTION STEP: BE ACTIVE IN LOCAL POLITICS

For Angela at Moon Palace, going to local meetings is an ethical obligation. She feels she must show up, for fear that her absence will mean the silencing of voices like hers. If she's not there, who will speak for the members of her community who share her values? I admire this attitude tremendously, and I hope for it to be widespread among people who believe in inclusion, literacy, and small businesses. The far right, an enemy of much that this book holds dear, has proven adept at taking school board seats and flooding public comment sessions. If nobody else shows up, they will have an unchecked path to implementing their harmful agenda. So many important decisions—from police budgets to library policy to what gets built (and how much money the developer gets from the government)—are made at the local level. Make sure your voice is heard in the room where those decisions are made.

At the bookstore level, how local governments incentivize businesses (and which businesses) can have a huge impact on neighborhoods and cities. Here's a scenario that's repeated itself time and again in American cities for more than a decade: Amazon decides to build a new fulfillment center and rolls into town promising thousands of new jobs. They politely ask for tax breaks wherever they can find them, and local governments are happy to oblige. This is not a way to protect bookstores and other small businesses. The American Booksellers Association (ABA) has reported that Amazon fulfillment centers have drastically displaced jobs and economic activity from downtown districts to industrial parks on the perimeters of towns and cities. The ABA provides a memorable illustration of this impact: Take the physical area and economic activity of the Mall of America. Multiply it by 300. That's how much economic activity Amazon's warehouses have displaced away from downtowns and into anonymous industrial parks on the outskirts.[71] If you find all this alarming, tell your local city councilperson. Make a phone call. Stop by city hall for a public comment explaining how important small businesses are. Write a letter, pen an op-ed, vote in local elections, do what you can to make it known to your local politicians that thriving small businesses (including bookstores) are important to you.

# CHAPTER 9:
# "NOTHING OF ANY VALUE
# HAS COME FROM A PLACE
# LIKE THIS"

## Two Dollar Radio Headquarters, Columbus, OH, and Biblioasis Bookshop, Windsor, ON

*D*riving down Parsons Avenue in southern Columbus, you wouldn't know it was the source of some of the best small-press literary fiction in America. Headed south on Parsons, a driver leaves behind the monstrous construction sites and new five-story apartment buildings that line the streets in neighborhoods to the north; absent are gastropubs and the slick brunch spots of the nearby Short North district. You won't find the painstakingly renovated row houses of the impeccable German Village here. As you drive past the gas stations, convenience stores, and taco trucks, pause when you get to the small branch of the Columbus Public Library at Parsons and Stewart. Look across the street to the little glass-fronted storefront building. There. That building is the source of books that can match or exceed anything that comes from a New York City high-rise. You can also find a vegan café and coffee shop in there, as well as a small but feisty selection of adventurous books for sale, nearly all of which are published by small presses. Welcome to Two Dollar Radio Headquarters.

Eric Obenauf and his wife Eliza, along with his brother Brian, started Two Dollar Radio as a publishing project in 2005. In the early days, the operation was modest enough that their only signage was a hand-painted piece of cardboard they propped in a window. Regardless of the humble roots, over the next few years they put out a striking and exciting list of books, from Scott McLanahan's *Crapalachia* to Hanif Abdurraqib's *They Can't Kill Us Until They Kill Us*. But even as Two Dollar Radio found its voice as a publisher, Eric and Eliza began to feel distanced from the books. He explains all this to me over cold brew at a repurposed vintage-store table in the back of Two Dollar Radio Headquarters' spacious and sunny dining area. He's lanky and tall, soft-spoken, and sporting his ever-present beat-up baseball cap. Despite being one of the most passionate and creative small-press publishers I've ever met, Eric basically has the demeanor of a surfer in the afternoon. Between sips of the cold brew, he tells me about losing touch with the passion for books the further Two Dollar Radio went as a publisher. He says that, eventually, "there wasn't that direct engagement with readers around books, and not even just exclusive to books that we published too." In the midst of this burnout, an idea formed: What about a bookstore? Eric explains,

> Nine or 10 years in, we were starting to feel beaten down, I guess, or a little estranged from the books and their life in the world too. And so the genesis for [the bookstore] was to have a physical footprint in the community where we could interact with people around books, community, and literary culture, because it was feeling pretty lonely where we were publishing books and throwing them out into the world.

At the same time that Eric and Eliza were having these thoughts, Donald Trump was racing to the presidency. "There was a lot of frustration and anxiety," Eric tells me, which led him to ask himself questions like "What are we actually doing in our community that's a greater force for good?" To answer that question, Eric and his team began to think about how they could go about "promoting different cultures, communities, ideas, races, ethnicities . . . a greater diversity of voices." It all culminated in a single idea: it was time to start a Two Dollar Radio bookstore. As he tells me, "We realized if we were ever going to do it, we should do it then. And so that was what spurred us to actually do it when we did it."

When to start a bookstore, and what kind of voice it should have, are two important questions. Another big one is the question of where. At the time, Eric and Eliza lived in a neighborhood "that purports to support Black Lives Matter and stuff like that, but there's no diversity at all." They weren't interested in that kind of performative activism. On top of that, a lot of Columbus's so-called "nicer" neighborhoods were out of reach; Eric explains, "We couldn't afford a lot of the neighborhoods while we were opening. We knew we needed a substantial footprint for the operations," requiring enough room for a kitchen, a dining area, a bookstore, and a warehouse to centralize Two Dollar Radio's publishing output. This forced them to be creative in where they looked. They eventually found Parsons Avenue, an area which Eric claims is 60% Black and 40% white. Eric and his team liked the idea of moving into a diverse neighborhood—it fit nicely with their bookselling and publishing philosophy—but he admits that doing so "opened a whole can of worms" because they didn't want to be "first-wave gentrifiers." The question of a white-owned business opening in a predominantly Black neighborhood is of course fraught, but at least the Two Dollar Radio team is thoughtfully engaging with what it means. For one thing, Eric and Eliza moved their family to the neighborhood, too: he points out the window as he tells me, "We live right around the corner. And that was important to us too, to actually live in the community where we work and have the storefront." For another thing, they're conscious of making the space as accessible as possible. As he enthusiastically describes a litany of past bookstore events, Eric says that the Two Dollar Radio Headquarters approach is "to give ownership over the space to basically anyone with a good idea for an event." He tells me about collaborations with Columbus City Schools. He tells me about sold-out events with all-star poets. He tells me about a concert by a local hip-hop star that turned into an onstage marriage proposal. Even if the question of a white-owned business opening in a majority-Black neighborhood still hovers over our conversation, Two Dollar Radio Headquarters is aware of it and working thoughtfully to become interwoven into its community.

Like so many other bookstores profiled in this book, Two Dollar Radio Headquarters had a difficult journey to where it is today. Unlike many others, Two Dollar Radio was actually able to secure a business loan to open their store. But the loan was tied to the terms of the store's lease. Eric had signed a three-year lease with four two-year extensions. That means Two Dollar Radio had to pay off the initial loan in three short years. To make it work, Eric tells me, "I was doing six days a week in the kitchen." While Eric was editing future bestseller and award-winner *They Can't Kill Us Until They Kill Us*, he was making vegan tacos and washing dishes late into the night to help pay off a short-term business loan. At the very same time, Columbus was preparing a proposal for Amazon's HQ2 competition that threw unspeakably huge incentives at the corporate giant, trying to lure them to town. Eric was elbows deep in suds as the city government promised Amazon no property taxes at all, on huge swaths of land, for decades. No such incentives were headed Eric's way, despite his honest and heartfelt efforts to build something meaningful in a neighborhood he would come to call home.

Fortunately, the store still stands to this day, and it's one of my favorite places in Ohio to hang out. Friendly welcomes echo out from Nathan at the ordering counter. High ceilings and huge windows let in beautiful natural light. Big wooden tables carry stacks and stacks of small-press books; instead of Random House, here you'll find Coffee House and Coach House and House of Anansi. Antique mismatched tables dot the space, letting folks have hushed conversations or work sessions pecking away at laptops. It's not a huge selection of books, but I still manage to find something surprising every time I go. That's by design, and it's one of the ways that being both a bookstore and a publisher creates synergy. Eric tells me, "That element of discoverability or exploration is what we tried to have in this space." To Eric, small bookstores are at their best when they're helping readers engage with cutting-edge small press literature. He tells me,

> I never understood Independent Bookstore Day where it seems like you're celebrating independent bookstores, but all the promotion stuff is the big authors, the big publishers, the really safe bets. I mean, it'd be the equivalent of having Indie Record Store Day and celebrating Britney Spears or something like that. It doesn't make sense to me.

Well, one of this year's Record Store Day releases is actually a record by Taylor Swift. Not to disparage Taylor (or Britney), but one of the real joys of joining a store's community is the ability to stumble upon something unexpected, something outside of the mainstream. Eric tells me, "If you're looking for cutting-edge and international literature, you're probably going to be getting it from a small press." There are a lot of good reasons for using bookstores as vehicles to promote that kind of book. To start, they can be really good at it, as evidenced by his work at Two Dollar Radio Headquarters. Additionally, it's a way to stick it to the corporate man; while cities fall all over themselves to lure the big corporations, a small-press purchase from a small bookstore is a way to double your support for people who represent the opposite of those corporations. As Eric says,

"When you buy a small press book from an indie bookstore, you're supporting two small businesses with one purchase."

·       ·       ·

When Daniel Wells decided to expand his business—Biblioasis Bookshop in Windsor, Ontario—to begin publishing books, he reached out to his former professor. The professor in question, one of Canada's leading historians of the book, had taught Dan Victorian history when he was in graduate school. Seeing as she was a scholar of the book, Dan was excited to tell her about his new project, broadening the horizon of his creaky used bookstore. But his news was not met with excitement. Instead, his professor was quite dismissive, as Dan tells me in his spacious office at the Biblioasis Publishing headquarters building. He pauses to take a sip of tea and then tells me that the professor told him, in as many words, "You could never be a publisher." She told Dan it would never work "for these reasons: you have no money, you have no experience. And, in the history of publishing, nothing of any value has come from a place like Windsor, Ontario. You simply can't amount to anything beyond a vanity press from a place like this."

On the wall behind Dan is a seven-foot-tall bookshelf absolutely crammed with the books that Dan and his team have published since 2004: Lucy Ellman's groundbreaking *Ducks, Newburyport*, for instance, which was shortlisted for the 2019 Booker Prize. There are books that were in the running for the Giller Prize and countless other awards. Bestsellers. Regional hits. Poetry. Books in translation. Local history. Wildly adventurous and innovative books. As Biblioasis has evolved from sleepy bookshop into Canadian small-press literary force, Dan Wells has never forgotten what that professor said. Through it all, he says his professor's dismissal "probably is the thing that kept me going." Indeed, Biblioasis's success (as bookstore and publisher) isn't in spite of Windsor, Ontario, but because of it.

When I ask Dan why he decided to start a bookstore, his answer is simple. He tells me, "Biblioasis opened in July 1998, in large measure because nobody would hire me." Nearing the end of a master's degree in literature, he was searching around for something to do. Repeated attempts to get hired at bookstores and libraries failed. Then, one day, he stumbled upon an auction house. Up for offer was what Dan calls "an incredible library of books." He tells me there were first editions by Ernest Hemingway, James Fenimore Cooper, and Tasha Tudor. He bought the whole thing for a hundred bucks. "I needed a break from school," he tells me, so he decided the auction library would be his bookshop. He never thought it would last. "I thought that I'd do it for a year. It would probably fail. My mother said it would fail. I'd get it out of my blood and I'd go on and I'd be an adult and be a scholar of the Scottish Enlightenment somewhere. But it didn't fail." To Dan, "the best thing about it is it opened up so many possibilities that wouldn't have been possible, especially in a place like Windsor, Ontario." Being in Windsor was an asset instead of a hindrance in one crucial way: it was close to the US. Dan tells me, "At that time, what kept me alive were American dealers," who would cross the border at Detroit to "root through the basement and spend thousands of dollars."

As Biblioasis Bookshop took hold, Dan began to broaden his participation in the greater Ontario literary culture. He spent time working on the Windsor Festival of the Book, which was cruising along for a while until the opening of an Indigo superstore "decimated" a lot of the area's small bookstores. Still, in his time with WFB, Dan "got a taste for literary promotion" and made connections with a lot of folks who would later take part in the Biblioasis story. Dan was slowly becoming more than a used bookseller. Another factor in Dan's transformation was the literal art of making books. He tells me, "Because I was an antiquarian bookseller, I was trying to figure out how to repair old books cheap. So I started taking book-binding classes and I fell in love with that. And after a while, I got tired of making blank notebooks. So I thought, 'Well, I'll start doing the odd pamphlet or chapbook.'" That's how the publishing part of Biblioasis started: handmade chapbooks. Dan reaches behind me to his monumental built-in bookcase and pulls out one of the first Biblioasis titles, a slim and absolutely gorgeous chapbook with a cloth spine and pressed cork cover. The paper is supple and luxurious, the printing is deep and clear. It's an amazing object. I had no idea. As I gawk over this beautiful book, Dan tells me, "All I wanted my entire life was to be involved in books in some capacity." With these handmade books, Dan was well on his way.

When he started selling that auction-house library, Dan was renting a space from a landlord who lived all the way in Toronto, more than 300 kilometers northeast. During the height of the 2008 recession, the landlord raised the rent to an unsustainable level, forcing Dan to close the physical space and convert his publishing and bookselling to online-only. "I decided," he says, "the only way I could ever proceed is if I could own the building." He set his sights on Walkerville, a historic industrial neighborhood that had fallen on some rough times. Despite the neighborhood's challenges, Dan had his heart set: "It's an incredible, incredibly important historic community. It was its own town." Eventually, Dan found a commercial building with two apartments that he could buy for a fairly low price of $160,000 CAD. He snatched it up. Again, this success isn't in spite of Windsor, it's because of it. Dan explains, "We can afford to take more risks here. Because you've got that margin already covered by having the cheap rent or owning your own building. Because my employees on an average publishing salary can buy a house. I mean, you can actually construct a livable life here as a bookseller and as a small-press employee in a way that just isn't possible anywhere else."

I'll pause here to say that Biblioasis Bookshop is a stunning place. After a long and at times uncertain history, this store is a total gem. It has old wood floors that instantly welcome even the chilliest reader. The sky-high shelves are absolutely stacked with one of the boldest, most innovative selections of books I've seen. Surprising, uncommon, and well-curated small-press books seem to be the bread and butter. Of course, Biblioasis titles play a prominent role, filling a tall pyramid-shaped display in the front window. But this isn't just the sales organ for the publishing part of Biblioasis; the bookstore is trying to accomplish much more, and it appears to this browser to be doing it quite well. If this is the kind of bookstore a place like Windsor can create, then Windsor should be celebrated.

One of the important ways that Windsor plays a role in Biblioasis's risk taking is the fact that it's in Canada, a place with key policy differences from the US. These differences make it easier for a place like Biblioasis Bookshop to exist. In the United States, many young professionals are entering fields like publishing and bookselling while carrying staggering amounts of student debt. In Canada, Dan tells me, "our education is so much more subsidized than yours. It's not that we don't leave school with student debt, but it's a fraction of what the average American student would receive." Dan was able to pay his way through school working as a welder at Chrysler; his lack of debt allowed his one-year auction-bought library experiment to turn into a celebrated, multi-decade career in bookselling and publishing. Another Canadian policy decision that makes it easier to make a career in Canadian bookselling is government-subsidized healthcare; again, Dan tells me, it's not free, and Biblioasis does offer health coverage for employees, but the whole thing is much less expensive in Canada than it is in the US. "I'm sure that plays a huge role" in why Biblioasis can do what it does, Dan tells me.

Yet another Canadian policy factor that makes Biblioasis possible is the government's direct support of Canadian publishing through government programs like the Canada Book Fund. Canada's government is much more involved than the US government in propping up the publishing industry, in part because, according to Dan, "Canadian publishing is in crisis." He tells me that, by title count, "Canadian publishers produce 85% of the books in this country," but, by sales, "Canadian publishers represent somewhere between 3 and 4.5% of the market." To stop the bleeding, the Canadian government has begun funding Canadian publishers and authors directly, including Biblioasis.

Dan certainly appreciates the help, of course, but he also claims that the publishing crisis the government is trying to help solve was caused in part by government policy. In the 1960s, Dan tells me,

> there were sort of cultural protection laws at the time. We realized, "We're next to the US and the US kind of dominates everything and everybody. And we're a very small market within the English language." There were these cultural protection laws that ensured that a native industry could build up. And then policies changed, or got ignored through the '80s and '90s as multinationals, who used to not have such direct access to the Canadian market, began to move in.

The cultural protection laws allowed iconic Canadian publishers like Coach House and House of Anansi Press to start. Eventually, though, the government caved to American and multinational corporations and the publishing industry plunged into crisis. So, the Canadian government implemented the Canada Book Fund, which, as of recently, provides funding for bookstores as well as authors and publishers. As of 2022, a new project of the Canada Book Fund offers grants to bookstores to update their technology. The amounts were calculated based on how many Canadian books a bookstore sold as a percentage of its total sales. Biblioasis Bookshop got around $6,000 CAD, which is not an earth-shattering amount of money. But it's still a lot more than an American bookstore has ever gotten from a bookstore-specific federal government support program.

So a few key factors have allowed Biblioasis Bookshop to exist for 25 years, eventually growing into an innovative and celebrated publishing house. For one thing, their unique location in Windsor, far from any cultural centers of publishing power, has shaped their success. For another, a few Canadian policies have allowed a business like Biblioasis to do what they do. Still another factor that allowed Biblioasis to continue was the fact that it's a publisher and bookstore at the same time. Just like his friends at Two Dollar Radio, Dan finds synergy in running both businesses simultaneously. It wasn't always that way, though; it took time to discover how the two arms of Biblioasis could work together. Dan tells me, "Figuring out how to manage both sides of this business has been really difficult. In the early days, I could be a publisher because the bookstore was paying for it. And then for a while, as my energy was directed almost exclusively into publishing, the bookstore began to fade. Now, I think we're reaching a point where they're both steadily on their own feet." Part of this balance comes from the fact that the bookstore is a hell of a lot more than just a place to sell Biblioasis-published titles: "For a while we were the only independent bookstore for 200 kilometers. So we've always wanted to be a community bookshop. I think a substantial majority of the people who buy Biblioasis books [from the bookstore] do not know that we're the ones who have published them." Indeed, the store has grown to function as a place for celebrating all independently published books, not just Biblioasis ones. Dan tells me, "The biggest issue facing independent publishing is the discoverability of our titles. This year we've done an experiment where we've been putting as many independent books face out on tables as we do the multinationals. And we've seen our independent sales increase to about 25 to 30% of our overall revenue when the average is 7." By this simple experiment in merchandising, Biblioasis Bookshop now sells four times as many books from small presses as the average bookstore. Not only does the bookshop help Dan advocate for small-press publishing in general, but it also makes him a better publisher. In addition to running Biblioasis Publishing, Dan does all the buying for the bookstore. This gives him access to real-time sales data that helps him "become aware of certain absences in the market. You begin to see what isn't there. So our Canadian history program has developed by seeing that this was a part of the market that was being abandoned by the multinationals. So there's that kind of symbiosis as well." Ultimately, with significant experience on both sides, Dan firmly believes that small bookstores and small publishers have an important relationship. He says, "If I have to rely on [big chain bookstores], I can no longer afford to take risks. Independent booksellers are the ones who allow us to say, 'Yeah, I can do that Icelandic translation. I can do that strange Irish memoir and know that if I find even 15 of you to sell it in your shops, we can probably make a go of it." He pauses, then says, "We are what makes each other unique."

Somehow, our time is already up. I guess if you get two booksellers with Rust Belt roots together, they can really get going. We decide to go get curry down the street. As he locks the door of the Biblioasis publishing office, one of two buildings he owns in this town, Dan reflects again on the professor who dismissed his publishing plans. Hands in pockets in the cold Canadian wind, he tells me, "She was, at that time, absolutely right. But here's what I didn't realize: everybody talks about the way the internet's changed publishing and changed bookselling, but one of the things that it made possible was for presses like us, or Two Dollar Radio, or many of the Minneapolis presses, to have a national and even international reach outside of those traditional publishing centers. And that's why Windsor became so essential to this story." I nod in agreement. "I used to run away from a regional focus because of that professor," he tells me. "But now it's my superpower."

· · ·

I paired Two Dollar Radio Headquarters and Biblioasis in this chapter because they share this: they're both publisher-bookstore hybrids, and they both do their amazing work in cities that aren't usually considered centers of literary culture. It was a natural fit; indeed, in each of their interviews, Dan and Eric, unprompted, mentioned the other fondly. These two stores have something figured out, and I think we can consider action steps by looking at what they do, where, and how. Based on our look at Two Dollar Radio, we can consider the importance of unique events and small-press book offerings. Then, taking our cue from Biblioasis and the way they've worked their location to their advantage, we can investigate some policies that lighten the financial load on bookstores.

## ACTION STEP: PARTICIPATE IN THE UNIQUENESS OF THE SMALL BOOKSTORE

Two Dollar Radio Headquarters takes great pride in how abundant and varied their event program is, with many events pushing the boundaries of what people think of as traditional literary events. Their event program is uniquely varied and wonderful, and if you're in Columbus or nearby I highly encourage you to take advantage of it. But nearly every bookstore does some kind of programming, and attending an event is not only a great way to protect that bookstore, but it's also most often a free thing to do. Attending an event makes you a part of that bookstore's community, and building a robust community is the bookstore's way of protecting its future. Additionally, the bookstore measures the success of events with the number of attendees, which often gets reported back to publishers. The publishers in turn look more kindly on bookstores that can provide big turnouts.

Apart from their great events, Two Dollar Radio Headquarters is also rightfully proud of its book selection, which is composed almost entirely of books published by independently owned small presses. Their inventory is a who's who of the translated, the surprising, the groundbreaking, and the weird. Even if they're not quite the small-press evangelists that Two Dollar Radio Headquarters are, a good bookstore won't carry the same books as a Walmart. You're much more likely to find translated books, small-press books, and otherwise offbeat or unique books at a bookstore. As Jason Guriel writes in *On Browsing* (a Biblioasis-published book), small bookstores "stacked the deck in favour of the quirky, the prickly, the heroically uncommercial. In favour of discovery."[72] This proclivity for off-the-beaten-path titles comes from the fact that bookstores are spaces that celebrate books, curated by people who love them. A good bookstore inventory specialist will lovingly work to fill their store with books that surprise and innovate. Sometimes, bookstores will collectively do this so well as to reverse-engineer an actual mainstream hit. Without the support of bookstores, Elena Ferrante's Neapolitan Novels wouldn't have found the massive mainstream audience they eventually did. Same goes for Robin Wall Kimmerer's now-classic *Braiding Sweetgrass*. Of note is the fact that both authors publish with independent small presses.

On a personal note, sales of *How to Resist Amazon and Why* far exceeded my wildest dreams thanks exclusively to bookstores' enthusiasm for the book (after all, there's no way it was a hit on Amazon). If readers show their hunger for weird, innovative, or surprising small-press books by buying them from bookstores, it's a clear message to the book industry at large that these books (and the stores that sell them) are important. Discovering and advocating for under-the-radar books is one of the most important functions of bookstores, and keeping demand high is a good way to protect bookstores and the work we do.

# ACTION STEP: POLICY TO LIGHTEN THE FINANCIAL WEIGHT ON BOOKSTORES

Dan at Biblioasis told me that one of the factors enabling their success was Canada's lower healthcare costs. In the US, health insurance and the cost of healthcare create a massive challenge for both bookstore owners and the people who work for them. It's a humongous expense—far too high. By some measures the US spends more money per capita on healthcare than anywhere else in the world.[73] How much is this a pain in the ass? Let me count the ways. First, bookstores operate on super thin margins, and offering health coverage for employees eats into that. Second, if health insurance is tied to employment, the natural incentive is to find jobs that offer it, and independent literary retail has a harder time affording it than other sectors. We're losing talented, passionate people because we can't pay for health insurance. And if a bookstore owner does offer health insurance, it might mean lower wages.

Let's get personal: I believe in offering the best possible jobs to the Raven's booksellers, even in the face of my industry's tight margins and lack of support for stores like mine. So, in 2019 I set out to offer health insurance. The messy business of trying to make that happen took me more than a year to figure out. A traditional group plan was far too expensive—simply out of reach if I wanted to offer plans that didn't have staggeringly high deductibles, or if I didn't want to cut wages. On top of that, for some of my employees, taking health coverage from the Raven would've *cost them money*. You see, the group plan would've been more expensive than plans they could get on the Affordable Care Act marketplace, but the mere act of my offering a group plan would've made them ineligible for those ACA plans! Basically, they would've needed to take a financial hit in order to get worse insurance. What we ended up settling on was something called an ICHRA, a plan that reimburses employees for their existing coverage. It's not nothing, but it's not ideal. I still have to ask employees to fight through the thicket of finding their own plans. On top of that, some of the plans offered by the ACA have high enough deductibles to be functionally useless.

The American healthcare system is beyond broken in so many ways; one of them is that it makes it very hard for bookstores to give their employees the health coverage they deserve. If everyone simply got universal single-payer health coverage from the government, it would alleviate so much stress and expense for small businesses. Talk about antitrust all you want (and if you've read this far, you know I certainly will), but the quickest, most pragmatic policy suggestion that would bring instant relief to every single bookstore? Universal healthcare. No question.

Another way for the government to lighten the financial burden faced by bookstores is, of course, to just give them money. As we've learned from Dan at Biblioasis, this isn't unheard of: the Canada Book Fund's first bookseller-supporting initiative awarded $12 million CAD to 180 booksellers, operating 467 locations, to better facilitate the selling of books online (this included that $6,000 grant to Biblioasis). All told, from 2012 to 2018, the CBF awarded $220.6 million CAD in grants and support, according to the Department of Canadian Heritage. Across the pond, the French government was highly active in giving bookstores money so they'd make it through the Covid pandemic, via initiatives like paying for the shipping of books during France's second lockdown. Both of these are perfectly clear examples of how the government can help protect bookstores by giving them money to help them solve their problems. But I can already hear the opposition to this idea: government spending is out of control. In response, a quick calculation. The CBF's $220 million CAD over six years equals about $37 million CAD a year. $37 million CAD is the cost of 7.5% of a single F-22 fighter jet. Six years of funding for the Canada

Book Fund is about one-fourth of what the NYPD spends on overtime in a single year.[74] Mind you, the US is a far larger country with a far higher GDP, so $37 million CAD a year wouldn't go quite as far here. Still, even that much would allow a lot of book dreams to come true while representing an insignificant cost for the government.

I should note that the US's National Endowment for the Arts does have literary initiatives. However, their funding goes to individual authors, as well as literary nonprofits. These are both worthy causes, for sure, but this structure makes it impossible for bookstores to directly benefit from NEA funding unless they're set up as a nonprofit. The clearest example I can give to illustrate the difference between how the Canadian government funds books and how the American government does it is this: Just now, when I looked at the copyright page of the nearest Canadian small-press book (Jason Guriel's *On Browsing* from Biblioasis), I saw an acknowledgement of the Canada Council for the Arts as well as a few other government agencies. On the copyright page of the nearest American small-press book (Saeed Jones's amazing *Alive at the End of the World* from Coffee House Press), I saw the NEA logo, yes, but also logos for Target and Amazon. Funding for a healthy book industry is crucial—so crucial, in fact, that we cannot leave it up to corporations.

A national book fund like Canada's, with its explicitly holistic focus on the entire book ecosystem, would protect American bookstores. Here's an easy first initiative for the hypothetical American Bookstore Fund: grants for new bookstores, with a special focus on booksellers from marginalized backgrounds. This would significantly reduce the bookstore industry's high-cost barrier to entry, which is the single biggest obstacle for the next generation of booksellers.

Government policy isn't the only policy that could lighten the load on bookstores. Publisher policy could do the same thing, perhaps even more effectively. Two Dollar Radio and Biblioasis have both found harmony as publisher-bookstore hybrids, but that doesn't mean all bookstores and all publishers have the most symbiotic relationship possible. One of the biggest reasons for bookstores' tight margins is the fact that most publishers offer lower-than-average wholesale discounts on books as compared to the rest of the retail industry. When a bookstore orders a book from a publisher, the average wholesale discount is 40–46%. Because of these discount rates, bookstores make less, as a percentage of the sale price, than many of our other retail peers. Publisher pricing is so bad that it's fairly common for Amazon to list popular books at or even below bookstores' wholesale prices. If a bookstore wants to sell a copy of N.K. Jemisin's new book *The World We Make*, the store writes a check to Hachette for $16.20 and sells it for the sticker price (which is printed right there on the book) of $30. Right now, Amazon is selling the book to consumers for $15.99. I'd never do it, of course, but it would actually be cheaper for me to order this book from Amazon than from the publisher wholesale. There are lots of policy suggestions that would solve this problem at the Amazon level. To solve it at the bookstore level, publishers could simply give better prices to bookstores. We hear all the time from publishers, sales reps, and publicists that bookstores are critical to publishers; though bookstores are a small market, publishers say, they're vital for things like discoverability and connecting with readers. One way publishers could prove their love of bookstores is to give bookstores a 10% better wholesale price. It would unlock lots of possibilities for bookstores, chief among them being to offer higher wages and better benefits.

# CHAPTER 10: "YOU CANNOT DREAM YOUR WAY OUT OF THINGS ALONE"

## Loyalty Bookstores, Washington, DC

*T*'m browsing quietly at Loyalty Bookstore. It's a January Thursday, right around noon, and the store has just opened. Loyalty is one of a few small businesses in a row of narrow storefronts on Upshur Street at 9th Street Northwest in the Petworth neighborhood of Washington, DC. I'm taken by this store's charm. Fancy but mismatched rugs line the floor, and old bookcases march along the walls. Posters and artifacts dot the top of the shelves, notably a giant check in the amount of $20,000 from *Good Morning America*, given to Loyalty in a splashy segment during the summer of 2022. Crammed onto the shelves are books almost entirely written by Black authors; a special section unofficially called "Sisters of Loyalty" stands right in front of the register, featuring the entire bibliographies of Octavia Butler, N.K. Jemisin, and bell hooks. The store feels broken-in in the best way. In a city filled with some of America's biggest and slickest bookstores, Loyalty feels comfortable. If DC's bookstores made up a house, this would be the cozy den, an impressive feat for a store that's less than five years old. I'm here to talk to the store's founder and owner, Hannah Oliver Depp, but I'd just as happily browse in here for a lazy hour or two.

The first thing Hannah says when they burst through the front doors is "Who wants coffee?" I raise my hand and so does Malik, the bookseller behind the register. Just as quickly as they burst through the door, Hannah bursts back out of it, dragging me in their wake to the aptly named Little Food Studio two doors down. In the space of about 50 feet, Hannah is already giving me a neighborhood tour, highlighting landmarks and people and other small businesses like they've been in the neighborhood forever. In a way, they have; a native of the Washington, DC, area, they now own and run Loyalty Bookstore locations in Petworth and Silver Spring, Maryland, both places that figured in their childhood. Not only does Hannah have connections to these places, but the places were, in their words, "neglected areas in the city that were crying out for bookstores." This is all the more meaningful because Hannah's bookselling career started at a large institutional bookstore in Washington, DC, that "was part of a neighborhood and community that really wasn't mine. Extremely affluent, a lot of just constant microaggressions, really exhausting." They tell me they "wanted to be part of a DC I felt more connected to and felt more at home at."

If our short walk down Upshur Street to Little Food Studio is any indication, Hannah's connection to the neighborhood is strong. Every bookstore owner I talked to for this book had to interrupt our talk to say hi to neighborhood folks, but I'm not sure anyone did it with as much gusto as Hannah does on this chilly, cloudy morning. The owner of Little Food Studio is sitting at a patio table working on their laptop, and the three of us have already discussed life as a small-business owner before the coffees are even ordered. Malik mentioned the sausage rolls, too, so we add those to the order. While we wait, we pass an extremely affable few minutes chatting and greeting passersby. I'm not sure there's a bigger joy in the world than spending time in a neighborhood with the owner of that neighborhood's bookstore. If neighborhood-focused bookselling is Hannah's goal, they sure seem to be on their way to accomplishing it.

Finally, coffee and sausage rolls in hand, we head back to Loyalty and the newly renovated children's section. Hannah sits on a vintage chaise lounge by the back window and I'm in a chair facing them. We're both self-identified neurodiverse booksellers, so we have to joke about the seating arrangement's resemblance to a therapy session before we get down to business. Once we get that out of the way, Hannah tells me the origin story of this vibrant, joyful neighborhood space. During their time at the large institutional store, despite their qualms about the neighborhood, Hannah still made good friends and connections in the industry. Doing so showed them "what the larger bookselling industry was and what its big flaws were and what it could be." But, in a traditional big-store model, Hannah could only dream about what bookselling could be. They say, "Pretty much the only two people at a store in the traditional model who have an influence over that are the owners and the buyer." Without a platform to fight for the book industry they wanted to manifest, Hannah got scrappy and searched out other options. As I reflect on Hannah's story, I admire their determination and tenacity, and I also think about how many other people with good ideas don't have a chance to make them real like Hannah has fought to do. Hannah tells me, in no uncertain terms, that it's "a huge institutional problem: that the people who know how to run bookstores can't afford to."

Hannah's first step was to move to New York and take a job at Brooklyn bookstore WORD, a small shop owned by former American Booksellers Association board president Christine Onorati. Christine took on a mentorship role for Hannah from the get-go; early in their time at WORD, Hannah told Christine, "I want to work for you for a few years and then I want to open my own store back here in DC." Rather than hesitating at the prospect, Christine leapt at the chance to mentor a next-generation bookseller. Later, when I ask her about this, Christine describes it as "the greatest honor I can imagine." For a bookseller to leave her store and go on to forge their own career in the industry is, in Christine's words, "fucking amazing. That's what we should hope for." Despite the mentorship and support from Christine, Hannah wasn't super keen on living in New York—"not my happy place," they tell me—but "the connections were invaluable." They did relish the chance to work at a newer, less-established store; Christine started WORD in 2007, when Hannah's former store had been in existence for decades already. At an institutional store like their first bookstore employer, Hannah says, "no one remembers how it is to be scrappy." Learning how to be scrappy would serve Hannah well in the next phase of their career.

"The idea for Loyalty started in 2014," Hannah tells me, but it would be four years before the store opened and another two before it reached the Petworth/Silver Spring configuration it has today. Initially, while working as Christine's "right hand," Hannah began to take business classes and connect with resources for young entrepreneurs. In the meantime, they started thinking about DC neighborhoods and running pop-ups when they could get out of New York ("My Amtrak points are still astronomical," they say). Eventually they fell into a consulting relationship with the owner of Petworth's Upshur Street Books. Things weren't going well at Upshur Street Books. Hannah tells me, "I was basically helping him figure out how to close without abandoning the neighborhood." The Upshur Street owner "was very, very passionate about the neighborhood. He had restaurants on the block, he really cared about this neighborhood, but he just over-extended himself. He was a restaurateur and didn't really understand the book side of things." Hannah decided they were in the right place at the right time, and that *they*, in fact, were the solution: "I decided I was going to try to buy his business." Hannah then embarked on a series of pop-ups to fund the sale, at the same time taking part in "a kind of work-to-own thing" at Upshur Street. To make the dream of Loyalty come true, Hannah spent six months with two bookstore jobs: one in Washington, DC, and one in Brooklyn. "I think I've probably been working seven days a week, 12 hours a day since 2018," they tell me.

Loyalty happened. Hannah did it. They've got two stores and big dreams for more. They've got a novelty check from *Good Morning America* to build a bookmobile. They casually mention a dream to buy a Baltimore warehouse to create an independent fulfillment center. In February 2023, Hannah launched a sweat-equity plan to bring on programs and marketing manager Christine Bollow as co-owner. But, even with all the hard work and the joyful Black exuberance of the Loyalty space, it's been far from smooth sailing. "I have been so unsafe in so many situations as the only Black person on the floor, as a female-presenting person on the floor, as a queer person on the floor," Hannah tells me. They continue,

> By opening a Black-focused bookstore, by being Black owned, we are automatically a target. We are a queer store with pride flags in the window. We are a target. Doesn't matter that we're in Washington, DC. First of all, Washington, DC, is a target. People come here, forget that we live here, think the entire thing is the Capitol, and literally piss on people's businesses and homes. They do not see us as people because of our different identities. They don't see us as people, but also being somebody who lives in DC, they don't think DC's a real place.

Hannah, like any owner of a Black bookstore, has to build safety and de-escalation concerns into their business model. "Consciousness of protection and community care is part of Black ownership," Hannah explains to me. To run a Black-owned bookstore, not to mention one in Washington, DC, is to spend time calculating threats and danger: "It is something I am constantly worried about and have no break from. It is in our mailboxes, it is in our email, it is on our voicemails, it is on our DMs. It is physically at our events." Nowhere was that more apparent than on July 16, 2022, when Hannah and crew had planned an outdoor Drag Story Hour in front of the Silver Spring Loyalty location.

Drag Story Hour was founded by author Michelle Tea in 2015 as a way to encourage literacy and curiosity among children. Loyalty has partnered with its local Drag Story Hour chapter since its inception. When the Covid pandemic began, Loyalty moved their Drag Story Hours outside whenever possible. The Silver Spring Loyalty location sits across the street from a pedestrian plaza, which had been a good place to hold events in a safe and socially distanced way. Loyalty's Drag Story Hours had gotten "a little bit of hate," according to Hannah, but nothing like the frightening and disruptive protests that began to spread across the country in summer 2022.

The pedestrian plaza across from the Silver Spring Loyalty location is owned by Montgomery County, Maryland, and it's operated by an association of downtown businesses. The county ownership means it's a public space, which makes things "a bit complicated," according to Hannah. Still, Loyalty had done some Drag Story Hours there without much fuss. But in the days leading up to the July installment, a group of far-right protestors showed up at the public library in town, causing Hannah and team to wonder if the protestors would target them next. Hannah began to prepare: "We contacted the landlords, we contacted the county, we contacted the cops, we contacted the [Downtown Silver Spring private] security team. And we said, 'Can there just be extra presence? We don't want cops. We just want there to be people who are clearly watching the situation because protest is fine, but escalation is not.'" If being prepared by contacting authorities helped put Hannah's mind at ease, that dispersed as soon as the event started: "When we got there, there were [security] people there. And then as soon as we started, the security presence walked away," they tell me. Whatever message needed to get to the security team didn't end up reaching them: Hannah says, "It was absolutely a miscommunication." Still, Hannah can't help but wonder if the problem was that "they weren't listening to me as the young Black [person] telling them what to do." Whatever security was needed at the event would have to be provided by Hannah and their booksellers.

Hannah and their booksellers weren't surprised when protestors showed up. At least initially, the plan was to carry on. To prepare for any protestors, they put a microphone on the drag queen, Logan Stone. Hannah explains that "originally we had Logan miked and we were like, 'We're just going to read through this.'" That worked for the first part of the story hour. After Logan had gotten through the first two books, though, the protestors started shouting. According to Hannah, they were yelling things like, "That's not a woman! Don't listen, kids! That's not a woman!" At the outset, the shouts didn't get much of a reaction from the crowd. Hannah says that the kids either didn't care whether the performer was a woman, or knew what it meant to be a drag queen and were fine with it. "That's not the point," Hannah says. But the lack of reaction to the initial shouts led to an escalation in the protest. Hannah explains that the protestors "started screaming about genitals and getting extremely graphic and threatening the amazing drag queen, Logan." As they did this, the protestors moved from the back of the event to form a line between the stage and the audience. The graphic verbal attacks, as well as the physically threatening move to the stage, caused both Logan and children in the audience to start crying. Hannah kicked into gear, and their team went from booksellers to security guards: Hannah tells me, "We asked all of the kids to walk down the block to the store. It's about a block away from where we were, straight shot. We're going to continue inside our store." This despite Covid concerns and the store's small space, not suited to such an event. Regardless, Hannah and team wanted to provide a safe space for these families and the outdoor plaza was no longer it. So Hannah escorted the "completely devastated and scared and very angry" families to the store to "chat and read." In the meantime, the other Loyalty booksellers escorted Logan to their car so they could safely drive away. If the protestors' goal was to disrupt a family story time, their goal was met.

Hannah wants to make it clear to me that they and their team are not against protest or dissenting points of view: they tell me the July Drag Story Hour "was not a situation where we wanted to keep them from speaking their pieces." The issue that caused Loyalty to pull the plug on the event was "when they got in the children's faces, and when they physically blocked off the exit for the drag queen." It's possible that this was the protestors' exact plan. GLAAD claims that there were more than 160 attacks on drag events in 2022 and early 2023, occurring in all but two states.[75] It would be naive to think these folks aren't sharing strategies and coordinating online in advance of their attacks.

Hannah's view on the situation is complicated, and like all of their bookselling philosophy, it's rooted in community care and anti-racism. According to Hannah's observations, most of the protestors appeared to be people of color speaking heavily accented English, leading her to think that at least some of them might be immigrants to the US. Hannah even recognized some of them, alleging that they "had come out and watched and surveyed in advance" at previous Loyalty events. But what Hannah found "extremely upsetting" was that, apparently, the leaders of the protest were two "white dudes . . . standing at the back of the event with their arms crossed" while everyone else put their bodies on the line to disrupt the event. Hannah's guess is that the people in the back with their arms crossed were pastors and the people blocking the stage were their congregants. On top of all this, the absent security team heard the shouting and rushed back to the stage. Hannah and their team knew this added another complication: any high-tension interaction between law enforcement and a group of brown people could turn ugly really fast. After they pause their recounting from the chaise lounge to catch their breath, Hannah explains to me, "Now I'm worried about these protestors, who were making me worried about the life of the drag queen, because now there's a security team layer and these are brown people."

At the end of her story, all I can say to Hannah is, "Wow." Of course, the reporting I had read about this incident lacked the nuance of Hannah's retelling, as well as the intersecting concerns for the safety of brown people in addition to the drag queen and the families in attendance. Before I could respond more fully, Hannah tells me, "That is what community care is. It's never simple. I'm worried about everybody."

In the aftermath of the July attack, Hannah and team were determined to carry on their Drag Story Hour program in a way that kept it free and safe for the performers and the families in the audience. To start, they stopped centering their security plan on police and private security teams. Hannah tells me that part of what led to the failures of security at the July event was their thinking that "I'm going to trust this institution instead of the community." Going forward, Loyalty's Drag Story Hours would have protection focused on community care. Hannah tells me that "once the story broke about all of this, the local queer community rose up and started a rainbow coalition to escort everybody into all the story times." These rainbow coalitions, a few of which have sprung up in response to Drag Story Hour attacks, create a physical barrier between the story hour event and any protestors that might show up, often forming a wall by lining up holding pride flags. One group, called the Parasol Patrol, creates a barrier with rainbow umbrellas. In some ways, according to Hannah, the attack caused a wake-up in the queer and leftist communities in their neighborhood, which suffered from what Hannah calls "armchair liberalism." They tell me, "The people had become really complacent . . . but once they figured out that this was going to be a consistent threat, they organized and it's been really lovely ever since."

While Hannah solved one problem by relying on community rather than institutional security, another arose: where to have the story hours in the first place. Both Loyalty locations are too small for the events as they existed, and the public plaza was clearly hard to control, not to mention fraught with painful memories for the families that were there on that July day. So they looked at renting off-site event spaces. That created problems of its own. For one thing, these facilities had rental fees, an added cost pinned on a business with tight margins. It also felt wrong, as an attack victim, to have to pay to prevent future attacks. Further, the venue owners got anxious when they heard about the rainbow coalition and Parasol Patrol. Hannah tells me they've fielded calls from venue owners saying things like, "Why is there a counterprotest? What's going to happen?" In response to this, Hannah tells me they've had to add the off-site events to their business insurance policy, another added cost. All of a sudden, a noble goal—to provide a free, family-safe, inclusive, literary environment for neighborhood families— had become expensive and dangerous. Still, Hannah tells me, "We're actually moving forward." It looks like the eventual path for Loyalty's Drag Story Hours will be to hold them in the stores. This necessitates renovation work, which is yet another cost: Hannah tells me, "I literally rearranged the store. We got different fixtures that are all on wheels so we can push them up against the walls" to make room for story time. On top of that, Hannah tells me with a sigh, "Well, it will have to be smaller. Yeah." But still, Hannah refuses to cede their ground. They tell me, with a laugh, that "even if it's costing me a week's worth of sales, which is technically a stupid business decision," they're going to carry on. "I'm just a stubborn asshole and you are not going to intimidate me out of doing Drag Queen Story Hour. It's not happening," Hannah says.

It didn't take long for Hannah's determination to be put to the test. On February 18, 2023, Loyalty held one of their new, smaller, indoor Drag Story Hours at their Silver Spring Location with drag queen Charlemagne Chateau. During the event, a group of protestors that included members of the Proud Boys tried to "force their way into our store during a Drag Queen Story Hour with physical violence," according to a tweet from Loyalty. Maryland Drag Story Hour events, including Loyalty's as described above, have long drawn protests but according to *MoCo360*, the February 18 event "appears to be the first time such a protest has involved violence."[76] Indeed, the scene got pretty ugly. As the Proud Boys and protestors tried to get into the store, the Parasol Patrol shielded the entrance with their umbrellas and chants. According to *MoCo360*,

> The protesters Saturday shouted anti-LGBTQ slurs and accused storytime organizers and counterprotesters— primarily a group called the Parasol Patrol DMV— of "grooming" children, according to video posted online and counterprotesters. They charged into counterprotesters, stomped on feet and punched one man in the face, the man, former County Council candidate John Zittrauer, told *MoCo360* . . . multiple people present at the event, including Zittrauer, reported injuries in interviews with *MoCo360* and provided photos.

Though the clash got bloody, the Proud Boys never made it into the store. Loyalty tweeted that the Parasol Patrol was able "to not only push back and hold the safe space, but to keep cheering and singing joyfully in the face of hate speech and disgusting threats." Ultimately, thanks to the Parasol Patrol's efforts to hold the line, "the children inside the store got to enjoy doing the Hokey Pokey, hearing beautiful books read aloud," Loyalty tweeted. It's all very intense, and it's hard to think of a scene that better captures the challenges of inclusive family programming for a Black-owned bookstore in 2023: inside, children are doing the Hokey Pokey in a joyful and inclusive environment, while outside, people have to physically fend off charging fascist protestors. If there's any doubt that bookstores need protection, consider this scene.

On their Twitter, Loyalty remained defiant as always, even in the face of their most violent protest yet. They wrote, "Loyalty will continue with our Drag Story Hour because A) it is an awesome time for kids (remember the kids? The ones enjoying being read to? This was supposed to be about them!) and B) because there is no hate or violence stronger than the love of our community." It's tempting to read a hopeful or at least useful note in this story: A beloved bookstore's Drag Story Hour was attacked multiple times but was repeatedly saved by quick thinking on the part of good booksellers. Throughout the sad saga, a formerly complacent leftist and queer community organized to use their bodies and voices to protect the store from more attacks. And that's all true. But it's also important to note that the bookstore has borne some pretty significant costs to respond to being attacked. Plus, they have ultimately ended up shrinking a popular and lovely program, giving fewer families access to an inclusive environment to enjoy books and each other. Those protest organizers, whether they're watching from afar with their arms crossed or punching Parasol Patrollers in the nose, still caused some serious pain to a group of people trying to do good and gentle work.

Hannah has seen many of the bookstore world's problems firsthand. They have found themself at a dead end, unable to advance their career at a legacy store. They have faced nearly impossible odds trying to open their own store. They have experienced micro- and not-so-micro aggression from customers and community members. They have been threatened and their store has been physically attacked. They have feared for their safety when trying to host an event. They have paid significant costs in moving on from that attack. Yet they remain idealistic, enthusiastic, and apparently committed to creating a better world for bookstores and booksellers. Like I've done in all my interviews for this book, I ask Hannah about solutions and paths forward. First, I ask them about those "armchair liberals." What should the well-meaning but complacent person do to protect booksellers and bookstores, not to mention books in general? Hannah's answer is simple: show up. According to them, the armchair liberals need

> to spend their money at the store. To request the books they want to see on the shelves at the library. To show up to these events. That's 80% of it. Honestly. Quite literally, if you are not showing up, especially at schools and libraries, they're just going to go with whoever the loudest voice is. If the only person showing up is the alt-right person who has been brainwashed, then the alt-right person gets to decide what's happening.

As for how to protect bookstores in general, Hannah's answer is just as elegantly simple: they tell me, "People are always like, 'Can we start a grant? Can we da da da?' I'm like, 'No, you just need to show up and shop. Yes, we need to lobby for better local business taxes and all of these things. Those are true, but for you as an individual, you just need to show up.'"

Where their vision for consumer action is simple and individual—just show up—their vision for bookstores is much more collective. Their impulse, which I think is shared by many, is to buckle down and try to fight your own way through it. They say, "I think this is the thing I'm bad at and I'm trying to work on this year. I fight my impulses every day to go into my corner and just figure it out by myself and then emerge with the brilliant solution." Being a business owner can be lonely. You can feel like the only solution is working yourself harder. As Hannah talks, I nod vigorously, hearing so much of myself in what they're saying. They continue:

I am trying to remember that you cannot dream your way out of things alone. So whether that is your booksellers, whether that is your community, whether that is your mom, or all of the above. Hopefully all of the above. We cannot dream our way out when all of us are dreaming in our corners.

Now it really is starting to feel like a therapy session. Even though Hannah's on the chaise and I'm in the chair, it's unclear who's benefitting from talking to whom. I chew on this thought and let a moment of silence sink in. As I take one last sip of that delicious coffee from the small and friendly café right down the street, Hannah says, "I have to remember that I am not the one who's going to come up with the solutions. But I can be the one to start conversations about finding them. Which is much harder."

·   ·   ·

Loyalty's story encapsulates so many themes of this book: The challenges of starting a bookstore, especially for young people from marginalized backgrounds. The importance of a bookstore to its neighborhood. The systemic problems in the book industry. But I'd argue the most urgent part of this story is Loyalty's tireless work providing inclusive programming for kids in the face of a highly mobilized and violent right-wing attack on their ability to do just that. Any store doing progressive, inclusive children's work has felt harassment and hate from the right; Loyalty and their activist community had to physically defend their space. Inclusive, welcoming children's programming and inventory is crucial for children and for bookstores. That's why it's crucial to defend bookstores like Loyalty from the right wing's attacks.

# ACTION STEP: BRING YOUR KIDS

In today's charged political climate, what and how kids read has become a culture-war flashpoint, and Loyalty is on the front lines. As I argue above, it's imperative for adults to protect family-friendly literary spaces from right-wing forces that are trying to limit what kids can read; in doing so, we are protecting the ability of all children to see themselves in books. But it's also important to let kids be kids and protect spaces where reading can be fun. How many people who run great bookstores today had safe spaces where they could fall in love with literacy as kids? I certainly did. Providing this space should be simple work, but it's becoming more fraught and dangerous by the day. But even if the fascists are charging outside, we must maintain spaces inside where kids can just read books and do the Hokey Pokey.

Aside from the urgent political work of protecting these spaces, catering to young readers is a good investment for bookstores. Given that bookstores rely on communities of readers, an important way to protect bookstores is to nurture young readers so they will remain readers as adults. If you'll allow me to get personal once again, I have a son who's four as of this writing. One of the greatest joys of parenting so far has been to share a love of books with him. I was afraid he'd somehow not care about books, but it turns out all it took to make him fall in love with reading was . . . reading. We made books part of his routine, making sure to read at least a few with him every day. We go to the library and let him pick out whatever he wants. We spend time in bookstores, of course. This is a wonderful rhyme of history, as the origin of my own story involves my Aunt Pat taking me to the Borders in Solon, Ohio. Every time Aunt Pat was in town, we went to Borders, and she made sure we didn't leave empty-handed. It doesn't even matter what the books were. I'd then return to a home where my parents regularly read to me, and later gave me plenty of space to read on my own. The joy of a beloved family member spending quality time with me surrounded by books was enough to hook me as a reader forever. Bring your kids to the bookstore; it's the best way to ensure they'll keep coming back. Unfortunately, this can take a bit more strategy these days (and even the involvement of local activist groups), but a good relationship between your kids and your bookstore is healthy for the kids and the bookstore alike.

# ACTION STEP: DEFEND BOOKSTORES FROM RIGHT-WING ATTACKS

The February 2023 attack on Loyalty wasn't an anomaly. Alarmingly, some recent right-wing attacks on bookstores are a lot bigger than some Proud Boys trying to force their way into story time, as dangerous as that was. In summer 2022, Virginia Republican politician Tommy Altman and his lawyer (and fellow Republican politician) Tim Anderson filed suit against Barnes & Noble. The alleged crime? Barnes & Noble simply carrying two books, Gender Queer and A Court of Mist and Fury. Anderson and Altman's suit claimed that the books were obscene and the stores needed parental consent before selling them to children. The suit was dismissed, but it represented a frightening escalation in a culture war that's raging across the country. In nearly every state, far-right reactionaries are working to prevent children from accessing certain books. These reactionaries have the endorsement of the national Republican Party in their efforts, and, as we've already seen in St. Marys, Kansas, they're also targeting libraries. It doesn't take Hercule Poirot to deduce that nearly all of the books in question feature queer characters or are written by queer, Black, Indigenous, or Latine authors. The right-wing reactionaries trying to take over public libraries and school boards in the name of "protecting children" are not protecting children at all. Instead, these reactionaries are trying to force a heterosexual, white, regressive worldview on children by limiting what they can read.

Just to be clear: using the government to limit speech is an obvious violation of the First Amendment, and it's happening right now across the country. Librarians are being harassed, threatened, and forced out of their jobs. In St. Marys and elsewhere, entire libraries are at risk of shutting down in the face of these coordinated attacks. While these bans give some already-famous books a sales bump, they make it harder for countless other debut or midlist authors to sell books, creating yet another barrier for queer and BIPOC authors. Most alarmingly, LGBTQIA+ and BIPOC kids have a harder time seeing themselves in books, which may contribute to the serious mental health crisis affecting these groups. It's not enough to wear a little button that says, "I read banned books." To protect bookstores, we need to end the right-wing attack on books, and you can't do that with lapel pins alone.

One actionable way to protect bookstores is to show up and literally get in the way. Of course, as a number of the anti-drag protests have become violent, not everybody will be comfortable putting their bodies on the line. Still, community organizing, whether that means literally standing on the front lines or not, is the answer to the attacks on libraries and bookstores. When Hannah was reflecting on the protest that disrupted their outdoor summer Drag Story Hour, they acknowledged that their failure was thinking, "I'm going to trust this institution instead of the community," believing that policing was the answer. The real answer, in their case, was connecting with grassroots efforts to protect childhood literacy and safe spaces. Months later, community activists, not security teams or police officers, prevented the Proud Boys from entering Loyalty and violently disrupting another story hour. This is a story that can repeat across the country, wherever people are trying to attack bookstores, and it's similar to the story of how to protect libraries that we learned about in Chapter 2: Show up. Maybe bring a rainbow umbrella or a song. This is how you protect bookstores.

# CHAPTER 11:
# "THE COMMUNITY IS PEOPLE"

## Source Booksellers, Detroit, MI

*D*uring my hour or so talking with Janet Webster Jones and Alyson Jones Turner, the mother-daughter duo behind Detroit's Source Booksellers, we're interrupted several times.

We're interrupted when a young couple Janet has never seen before comes into the store looking curious. Janet leaps to her feet, faster than I'd expect a woman her age to do anything. But that's just unfairness on my part. If I had Janet's energy, I'd be leaping to my feet too. Janet welcomes the new couple to the store and begins asking them questions about their lives. Soon, mutual acquaintances are discovered. Books are recommended, thank-yous are exchanged. Janet has big hugs for these people she had presumably never seen before.

Other times, grandchildren are asked after. She asks people about the classes they're taking. A spontaneous discussion pops up about the difference between the male gaze and the female gaze in photography. The postal carrier is heartily greeted by name.

At another point, Janet pauses our interview to sing the goodbye song from *The Sound of Music* to a group of departing customers. When Janet returns to her seat at the corner table where we're camped out around my tape recorder, nobody can remember what we had been talking about.

This happens several more times during the interview. Sometimes I'm the distraction, as Janet interrupts her own train of thought to all but yank me out of my chair to show me something across the store. The fiction shelf, for instance, a new development in a store that's made its name selling nonfiction. A stack of books for a large off-site event. A graphic novel about an important but overlooked part of Detroit's history. If the interviews for this book had step counts, this one would win.

Always, when the interview resumes, Janet and Alyson finish each other's sentences in a way that only a mother and daughter can. This is perhaps exacerbated by the fact that Janet and Alyson have worked closely together for a long time. An example exchange:

Janet: So we were identified by Midtown Detroit, Inc., which is our big umbrella business.

Alyson: For the cultural center.

Janet: Business, community development, and preservation organization, for this space that rests between all four expressways and houses, the entire cultural center, or I like to say the heart of Detroit.

Alyson: Which would be the main library that's 150 years old, the Detroit Institute of the Arts.

Janet: African American Museum, the Historical Museum, Wayne State University, the medical center.

Alyson: The medical center. This is all . . .

Janet: Residents Gallery and all that.

Me: (trying, but not too hard, to get a word in edgewise) It's all within the four. . . . It's the . . .

Janet: Between the four expressways. That's the way they like to put it.

It's a bit dizzying to try to keep up with this back-and-forth, but it's certainly fun, and it's nothing if not welcoming. I sit across the tiny table from both of them, in the heart of this small bookstore, and warmth just emanates outward. And it's not because they already know me, or because they know I'm working on a book about bookstores. Janet and Alyson emanate the same warmth and welcome to every person who walks in the door while I'm there—their booksellers, their delivery drivers, their customers. This tiny bookstore tucked into a commercial strip in a fast-changing Detroit neighborhood is a locus of community, care, and warmth. And it just may hold some answers to this book's central questions.

•　　•　　•

Janet Webster Jones founded Source Booksellers in Midtown Detroit in 1989, making it one of the Midwest's oldest Black-owned bookstores. Originally, Janet operated Source as what she calls a "vendor," bringing tables of books to Detroit events and places where community was already gathering. Don't call it a pop-up, though. When I utter the term, Janet responds, "There's a big difference between a vendor and a pop-up. Vendors go to where people are gathered. And I would go to where people had gathered for different reasons." To Janet, at least, it seems like this is the distinction: even though a pop-up bookstore is temporary, it's still rooted in one place. Despite its short-term nature, the idea of a pop-up is still that you put books in one place and wait for people to show up. I think Janet forcefully corrected me in this notion because her start in bookselling was rooted in the opposite: she brought books to where people *already were*. Rather than wait for people to show up, Janet did the showing up. I think this is central to her bookselling philosophy to this day, even though Source has long since moved into permanent digs. Animated as always, Janet continues: "We made ourselves available to where people were. We didn't go sit down somewhere and wait for people to come. It always seemed strange to me that people would do that." When I ask how this roving community-following philosophy has changed since Source moved to a permanent brick-and-mortar model, Janet replies, "I always say our mission is to serve the community. Who is the community? Anybody who has the courage either to walk in the door, or invites us to go somewhere." This expansive definition of community is embodied by Source's impressive roster of off-site events, places where they act more like the vendor of 1989 and less like a bookstore in a building. Throughout our conversation, they mention numerous churches, Kwanzaa celebrations, and all kinds of fairs and bazaars, as well as both the Lions Club and the Detroit Lions. This small bookstore, though it's found a permanent home, still has connections to its vendor roots, connections that animate its philosophy of community.

Actually, the small bookstore isn't quite as small as it used to be. In 2002, Janet retired from her job at Detroit Public Schools and decided to devote more time to Source. She and a few other folks formed the Spiral Collective, a group of Black woman–owned businesses in Detroit's Midtown neighborhood, right across the street from Source's current home. After growing the business even further, Janet moved Source across Cass Avenue to its current spot in 2013. In 2021, the store expanded into the vacant adjacent storefront with the help of grant support, not an easy thing for a for-profit business to pursue. Still, Source figured it out. Funding for their expansion came from two sources: first, economic development nonprofit Midtown Detroit, Inc., started a program that identified and supported neighborhood anchor stores within the Midtown area. Source got the anchor designation, and the associated support. As Janet tells me, "I'm the anchor store in this area. That anchor designation brought money and the money allowed us to have the demolition done . . . and the construction of what we wanted next door." Second, they received a Survive to Thrive grant from the Book Industry Charitable Foundation (BINC). According to BINC's website, Survive to Thrive was a program designed to support bookstores "that have been able to adapt throughout the pandemic and have community-minded innovation plans going forward." Janet was hesitant to apply; she knew lots of folks who worked for BINC and had even coordinated fundraising efforts for them in the past. But a friend at BINC told Janet, "You better apply," and the judging was done by a neutral third party anyway, so she did. Together with the Midtown Detroit support, the Survive to Thrive grant paid for Source to double in size. Alyson says the expansion would've been impossible without the grant support: "Yeah. We couldn't have done it without it." Janet chimes in, gesturing to the new room next door, "You can't sell enough books to do that." They tell me Source has always been self-sustaining in the sense that book sales are enough to pay for payroll and ordering more books, but the margins of the business made expansion plans impossible without external support. Two external groups rightly pointed at Source and saw an anchor business serving a vital role in its community, and pledged it support without any expectation of being repaid. If only there were more investment like this in the small businesses driving their communities.

In my rambling, exceedingly pleasant discussion with Alyson and Janet, the idea of community keeps coming up. This is normal for booksellers—for instance, when I do job interviews, I often track how long it takes for the applicant to first say the word "community." But Alyson and Janet seem more committed to the idea than most. They identify with the broader Black-owned bookstore movement, but they also strongly identify with their own community in Detroit. Janet tells me,

> So I think that we're always a little bit cautious when people say, "Oh, you're a Black bookstore." I say, "Yeah, we're Black." We've been colored, negro, Black, African American. We've been all that. And we are also booksellers. And our bookseller identity is that we serve the community and we have a strong thread of African

American materials. And we're a nonfiction bookstore.

All of that is part of our identity.

Black bookselling is a part of who Source is, but they wouldn't want me to let you forget that community is part of their identity too.

What "community" means along Cass Avenue in Detroit is an interesting discussion these days. Detroit is changing, and in few places is it more evident than along the so-called Cass Corridor. Two years after Janet and Alyson moved Source into its own storefront on Cass, Jack White opened his vast, shiny new Third Man Records store and record-pressing plant around the corner. The flagship Shinola store is nearby. Brewpubs and restaurants and new apartments keep appearing. It's not easy to find parking, and I have to pay for it when I do. In a city still actively grappling with the devastating effects of population decline and industrial collapse, where entire neighborhoods are vacant or nearly so, Cass Avenue is a hub for new construction, economic activity, and energy. Some may see it as economic development finally returning to a city that has been starving for it for half a century. Others may see it as gentrification, outsiders swooping in to build new housing that longtime neighborhood residents can't afford. I'd be remiss in not asking Janet and Alyson about this, since they're longtime neighborhood residents running a business in the very heart of whatever's happening along Cass. But when I ask them about it, they bring it right back to their notion of serving the community. They're just serving a changing community. I ask Janet about how the Midtown neighborhoods are different these days, and she replies, "Well, they look different every day. That's part of what life is, it's changeable, and it's different from what?" I press a little bit, mentioning Third Man and all the new buildings and businesses along Cass and elsewhere in Midtown. That prompts this exchange, with Alyson's constant laughing bubbling in the background:

Janet: It used to be raggedy, torn down, pornographic. Is that right? Pornographic and drunk, and everything. And before that, it was a well-established neighborhood.

Bookseller on duty: (chiming in from the front desk) Circle of life.

Janet: (singing) *Circle of life.* That's from *The Lion King.*

Alyson: Okay, Ma. Okay.

To Janet and Alyson, the current wave of development (or gentrification) isn't the end or the beginning of the story of Detroit, or Midtown. Source is and always has been a bookstore trying to adapt to seismic changes shaping its neighborhood. Highway projects have displaced huge and essential Black communities. Neighborhoods go from vibrant to rundown and back. Demographic and economic forces shape the city, and marginalized people often feel the brunt of it. It's part of the story of Detroit. Janet tells me,

> Those changes are always occurring and the demographics are always happening. Now we have this movement of people coming from the coasts, both East and West, and the southern coast, because of climate. And we're going to have more refugees coming. When I was a child in high school, the big happening with the Soviet Union was the absorption of Lithuania, Estonia, and the other one. But people came here.

People move. Neighborhoods change. Cities are shaped by crisis and migration and geopolitical events and highways and trains. Amidst this larger story of Detroit, a community bookstore needs to adapt and find ways to serve neighborhoods shaped by huge external forces. Alyson chimes in on the importance of continuing their community-oriented bookselling work through changing times: "Luckily, because we've been around for 33 years, people can find us and get their books. I don't think we have that much of a loss of people, but I think where they live might have changed, that they may have been pushed out or have to come from a longer distance or we have to send it to them or something like that." This is an idea well suited to Source's long-held vendor-inspired notion of going to where people are already gathering. As the neighborhood changes, the places where Source needs to go to meet their community may change too, but their commitment to doing so will not. Perhaps one small bookstore cannot stop seismic changes to their community, but they can definitely adapt their work to better fit a changing community's needs.

As I've already touched on, it's nearly universal to hear booksellers talk about serving their community. I think it's rare for a good bookseller to *not* ground their practice in community, at least a little bit. But I often wonder, what exactly does that mean? How exactly does a bookstore *build* community? How does a bookstore *serve* community? I don't think any of those questions has a single answer, but I'm not sure anyone puts it as clearly as Janet does when she tells me, "The community is people, and the people are the customers, and we want to serve them in all kinds of ways." It seems so simple, but there's so much to that idea. Maybe that's why Janet and Alyson are so reluctant to make sweeping statements about the State of Midtown. The readers of Detroit are still people, and as far as Janet and Alyson are concerned, their bookstore's job is to serve those people in lots of different ways.

Source has a big toolkit for accomplishing this. They team up with all kinds of local organizations and nonprofits. They shift their inventory based on what people are looking for— they're expanding a bit more into fiction and Black mysticism and children's books. They leaned hard on online ordering and shipping during the pandemic. But, after spending time at the store, it seems like one of the biggest ways they serve community is by just providing an open door and a friendly welcome. Janet tells me, simply yet profoundly, "I think that bookstores should be welcoming." As I return to the interview transcript to write this chapter, I'm reminded again of how cheerfully and frequently Janet and Alyson interrupted themselves to greet customers, often by name, at times asking after family members. When I ask her to elaborate her thoughts on why bookstores should be welcoming, Janet explains, "The bookstore doesn't demand that you buy something. . . . I'm not here so that you just have to buy. This isn't like 7-Eleven where you grab a pop and go. You don't have to do that. You can come in here and look around." It's a store, yes, so selling books is part of what keeps their lights on. But Janet and Alyson trust that that'll happen, and they remain focused on being welcoming neighbors before they're salespeople.

Every bookstore says they're about their community, but it seems like Source has thought about how to do that more than the rest of us. After all, their literal start came from bringing tables of books to places community was already gathered. Community work is so important to Alyson and Janet, in fact, that it's an important part of how they define being a bookstore in the first place. Maybe even more important than the books. Janet tells me that a bookstore "can't be just a vehicle for publishers passing books through you. It can't be that because the community is the place where you're sitting, the people you want to serve." A bookstore is not just a mechanism for shuttling books from publisher to consumer. That's what Amazon is, and its book-buying experience is joyless, scattershot, and bleak. The very thing that makes a bookstore more engaging, vibrant, and enjoyable—the very thing that makes a bookstore a bookstore—is its connection to its community.

When we're all wrapped up, Janet won't let me leave. She keeps showing me new parts of the store, telling me new stories. She starts just handing me books that I "need to read."

It feels like I'm being handed dishes of leftovers after a family gathering. I really need to get going, but I don't quite want to.

• • •

I'm concluding with Source's story because they demonstrate an important truth about the work that bookstores do: without some consideration of community, a bookstore is just a funnel between publisher and consumer. It follows that whatever magic a bookstore has comes from that consideration. The action steps that we can take away from Source's story, then, are about community: both viewing your business patronage holistically, and taking steps to organize for better communities.

## ACTION STEP: SPEND TIME WANDERING THE NEIGHBORHOOD

Alyson and Janet have a holistic view of Midtown Detroit: to them, the neighborhood is evolving and their bookselling practice is evolving along with it. I think this perspective can inform consumers and entrepreneurs in a way that protects bookstores.

To demonstrate, a quick story: After a series of increasingly aggressive sales calls from online review aggregator Yelp, I broke down and finally listened to their pitch. They wanted me to pay $25,000 a year for advertising to ensure the Raven appeared first in Yelp search results. Thus, we'd appear above what they considered our competition, the Dusty Bookshelf down the street. We said no. First of all, our entire yearly marketing budget, which we calculate based on industry averages, is less than half of $25,000. Second, of course, we don't view the Dusty Bookshelf as our competition. This is a key difference between the Silicon Valley view of things (Yelp) and the small-business view of things (the Raven or Source): we believe that if our neighbor businesses are thriving, so are we. We are rooting for all the other shops and restaurants on our street because our business model is built on a steady stream of traffic past (and hopefully through) our door. A great way to build that traffic is to have lots of small businesses in a small area of town. So here's another cheap and easy way to protect bookstores: go downtown and wander.

## ACTION STEP: LINK UP WITH ORGANIZATIONS WHO ARE DOING THE WORK

One of the ways that Source evolved to serve their evolving neighborhood was their recent expansion into the storefront next door. It allowed them to broaden their inventory to reflect their community's interests, and it provided space for the infrastructure required for them to meet people where they were already gathering. The expansion would have been impossible without a grant from BINC, the Book Industry Charitable Foundation. According to its website, BINC was founded with a mission of "assisting bookstore employees & comic retailers facing hardship & supporting career development." Any bookseller facing any kind of financial hardship can apply for BINC funds; the process is easy and fast. They also offer large-scale support to bookstores, like the Survive to Thrive program that allowed Source to expand. I've watched multiple Raven booksellers receive life-changing help from BINC. Yes, BINC accepts donations. This is one of the most direct ways to protect bookstores.

And it doesn't end with BINC. Fortunately, there are a ton of other great organizations fighting for the kind of world where bookstores can thrive. One way to protect bookstores is to link up with those groups. Organizing and coalition building is an effective method for creating change, especially when the gears of policymaking move too slowly. In *Chokepoint Capitalism*, Rebecca Giblin and Cory Doctorow write, "The most important individual action you can take is to join a movement."[77] In the introduction to this book, I mentioned how bookstores can introduce people to social movements because they're more durable than movement spaces like protests or occupations. Another entry point to social movements (like, for instance, a movement to protect bookstores and downtowns and small businesses and freedom of speech) is linking up with organizations that have a long history of activism. If you're concerned about the issues presented in this book, and if you're committed to protecting bookstores, below is a list of some organizations that are already doing good work. There's no single action that translates to support for every one of these organizations, but following them on social media and subscribing to their mailing lists is a great start. From there, let them tell you the ways they need support.

- **The American Booksellers Association** has, for more than a century, advocated to protect and enrich bookstores and the people who work in them. The ABA has a long history of pushing a pro-small-business policy agenda, from suing to fight unfair chain-bookstore pricing practices in the 1990s to being a leading voice in the new antitrust movement today.

- **Athena** is a coalition of labor organizations working to raise awareness about (and fight) Amazon's predatory practices.

- According to its website, the **Institute for Local Self-Reliance** is a think tank that "builds local power to fight corporate control," with focuses in antitrust, small business, local utility control, local broadband, and more. Their work has been instrumental in writing both this book and *How to Resist Amazon and Why*.

- **PEN America** and the **National Coalition Against Censorship** are two groups working to combat the right-wing attack on freedom of speech.

# CONCLUSION: FINDING MORE QUESTIONS

*T*he question that started me down the road to writing this book was this: How *exactly* do bookstores build community? After years of talking about bookstores and community in vague terms, I found myself wanting specifics. I had an idea that there was a story there, and I was not wrong. I actually found 12 stories, and I'm sure there are countless more. Now that I'm on the other side of a year of traveling around to talk to booksellers, doing dozens of interviews and studying hours and hours of transcripts, I'm both closer to and further from the specifics I was hunting. For every answer I found, I found myself asking two or three more questions.

I'll get to the questions in a minute, but for now, the answers. How does a bookstore build community? The simplest answer is that a bookstore provides economic value to its community. It's important not to forget that. Bookstores create jobs, keep money in the economy, and help to define local character. There's even evidence that bookstores do this more effectively than other small businesses. While this work is important, there are more complicated and essential ways that bookstores build community, too. Now that I'm at the end of this investigation, I've found that these 12 bookstores demonstrate, loosely, four specific ways that bookstores build community.

First, a bookstore can build community by fighting for justice. Indeed, it can be argued that a bookstore is a small business uniquely suited to fighting for a better world. At the base level, the decision about what to put on the shelves and how to curate the physical space of the store is a way to make a political statement. Every bookstore in this book is engaged in that political work. But a bookstore can also build community through justice work that extends beyond the shelf. Moon Palace, thrust into the literal center of the turmoil surrounding George Floyd's murder, became an abolitionist voice in their community. Their work ranged from practical actions, like feeding free pizza to protestors, to long-term advocacy, like making sure to show up as an abolitionist voice in discussions of the future of the neighborhood. Across town, Birchbark addresses economic injustice by providing a place for Native artists to sell their work at a fair price. They also advocate for Native books, languages, and learning by acting as a hub for the Indigenous community in Minneapolis and the greater Midwest. Another Midwestern author-owned store, Bookends & Beginnings, has been in a political "battle for the soul of Evanston" for years. That political work ranges from advocating for commercial renters' rights to launching an antitrust suit against Amazon. All bookselling is political, but some stores adeptly leverage that political work into creating, building, and nurturing community.

Other stores focus on workers and the issues facing them. In doing everything they can to create a just and fair workplace, even in an industry that has historically provided neither, these stores build community by building a good place to work. At Red Emma's, that means a clear pathway to becoming a worker owner for everyone who works at the store. On top of that, it also means creating lasting systems that will help them export their worker-owned co-op model to other businesses. At Avid, it means taking a stand on behalf of queer employees when queer books come under attack. It also means providing as many benefits as possible, like a generous family leave policy. But building a just workplace isn't only about benefits; Avid employees know their emotional health is important because they have space in regular staff check-in meetings to talk about it if they want to. Both stores are public and outspoken about their work creating a good workplace, and I think that's the community-building part: providing a good workplace is important, but advocating for others to do the same is how a store can help create widespread change.

Let's not forget that a bookstore can build community through the books themselves. Nobody is better suited to create and nurture a literary community than a group of talented booksellers. On a broad scale, bookstores across the country and around the world are doing valuable work to help readers discover literature, and to advocate for unique and overlooked books. Nowhere is this more apparent than at both of the bookseller-publishers featured in this book, Two Dollar Radio and Biblioasis. Both are laboring tirelessly to put innovative and surprising books into the world, through what they publish and what they sell in their bookstores. As a bonus, they're doing this in cities that are typically overlooked as literary hubs. Elsewhere in the Midwest, A Room of One's Own is passionately pushing their selection of trans-ecstatic books, and Semicolon is doing everything they can, despite near-constant challenges, to celebrate the intersection of Black books and Black art. These stores all demonstrate that joyful, enthusiastic bookselling can build and animate literary communities more effectively than almost anything else.

Frighteningly, lots of folks on the political right are threatening that literary joy through protest, policy, and even violence. That's why the fourth way bookstores build community is so crucial: bookstores not only build literary communities, but they also fight to maintain a safe and welcoming space for those communities to gather. This could mean the warm welcome of a greeting from Alyson and Janet at Source. This could mean 60 years of providing a safe and warm bed for thousands of writers, like Shakespeare and Company is doing to this day. This could mean mobilizing your community to physically defend your space like Loyalty did, fending off the Proud Boys so the kids inside could keep doing the Hokey Pokey. I think this is the clearest demonstration of the importance of a safe space for kids to gather: these are spaces where kids can be themselves and fall in love with books. Hopefully this book has convinced you that they're worth protecting.

It's not just these 12 stores that are building community. It's not just these 12 stores that are facing challenges and even danger in doing that work. Every bookstore is functioning both in micro and macro. Yes, much of the work of a bookstore is local, and that's a good thing. But each of these individual stories is happening in the midst of a bigger story facing all bookstores: Amazon is gobbling up a significant majority of the book industry with their predatory practices. Commercial rents are sky high and climbing. Antitrust enforcement, though finally showing signs of waking up, has been largely hibernating for the last four decades. And, crucially, the bookstore business model is set up so that it's incredibly hard to properly compensate the people doing this difficult but vital work. It remains a steep challenge to make a career in bookselling, especially for those who don't already have money. Still, these booksellers are building community despite the massive challenges in their path. It all makes me wonder what could be done if bookstores *didn't* face such steep odds just to stay open, let alone do the innovative and inspiring community work discussed in this book. What if the world functioned in a way that made it easier, not harder, for bookstores to do what they do so well?

In addition to imagining a better world for bookstores, another piece of the puzzle is imagining how bookstores themselves can be reinvented to enable a thriving future for books, booksellers, and communities. Envisioning a bold future for bookstores is vital, because "continual repurposing" (to borrow Kimberly Kinder's phrase) could be a path towards sustainability. I suspect an entire book could be written on this alone, but below are some of the questions I found myself asking about the future of bookstores. To highlight the issues raised by these questions, I've provided a few anecdotes from some bookstores that aren't profiled in this book. By including brief stories from some other stores, I want to show two things: First, the 12 bookstores profiled in this book aren't the only ones doing interesting things. Second, the issues facing bookstores, and the questions they inspire, have broad implications for all bookstores and the communities who love them.

- *Can we find innovative paths to building ownership to eliminate reliance on landlords?* The queer feminist co-op Firestorm Books in Asheville, North Carolina, recently used crowdfunding to purchase a building. Immediately, they donated the land to a land trust, ensuring that predatory developers will never be able to build there.

- *Do bookstores need to be for-profit businesses?* Chicago's Seminary Co-op reinvented itself as a not-for-profit entity, the only nonprofit whose mission is selling books. Buffalo Street Books in Ithaca, New York, is a customer-owned co-op. Word Up Community Bookshop in Washington Heights, New York, is a 501(c)(3) nonprofit operated by a small staff alongside dozens of neighborhood volunteers. A feisty handful of radical co-op bookstores, like New York City's Bluestockings, sell books outside of the traditional for-profit model. Many other bookstores, like St. Louis's Left Bank Books, have affiliated nonprofit entities that help further their missions.

- *Do bookstores need to be in one permanent location?* Sure, one of this book's central ideas is that a bookstore's permanence makes it valuable for activist organizing. But is there also value in being able to meet communities where they already are?

Cincinnati's Book Bus roves from festival to festival selling books, parking in a bookstore-garage hybrid permanent location in the offseason. Other stores are mobile-only; for instance, Milwaukee's La Revo Books draws from the Mexican mercado tradition to meet their customers at the community events where they're already gathering.

- *How can bookstores be accessible to all people, regardless of ability?* How many bookstores have stairs at the entrance, for instance, or don't have public restrooms? It's common to hear bookstores talk about welcoming and accessibility, but it's much rarer to find a bookstore that's accessible for people with disabilities. Black Garnet Books, Minnesota's only Black-owned bookstore, made accessibility a central focus when opening their new brick-and-mortar location, with a stated goal to not only meet but exceed ADA standards for physical spaces.[78] Their efforts included using crowdfunded money to pay for a $5,000 power door, representing a community investment in accessibility. What does a world look like where all bookstores are accessible to people of all abilities? What about a world where the onus to pay for these accommodations isn't on already-stretched small-business owners? What does a world look like where it's easy for disabled people not only to shop at bookstores, but also to work at them?

- *Do bookstores even need to sell books?* Rapper Noname expanded her popular online social justice book club into the Radical Hood Library, a worker-owned LA storefront lending library. Radical lending libraries are interesting to me; the SWAP Book Co-op in Oberlin, for instance, allows students to get textbooks for free in exchange for book donations or shifts manning the "store." Then there's Gainesville's Civic Media Center, a radical lending library focusing on zines. Can a radical lending library do the same community work as a bookstore without forcing radical activists to operate within capitalism? And can a radical library give away reading material for free and still fairly compensate the workers making it happen?

- *Can booksellers also be bookstore owners?* This book spends time investigating the employee-owned co-op model, but there may be other models for employee ownership, too. In 2018, the owner of Porter Square Books concocted a plan to sell 49% of his store's ownership interest to a group of longtime employees. In 2022, we implemented a similar plan at the Raven—one of our attempts to make bookselling into a sustainable career.

- *Is "indie" even the right move?* It's long been a habit to call local, non-chain bookstores "independent bookstores," and I certainly understand that impulse. I address my issues with this term in the introduction, but I also think moving beyond "indie" might allow for the dream of something bigger. What if bookstores aimed for collectivity rather than independence? That could look like collective ownership and the rise of a business model that no longer relies on the use and regeneration of a single person's wealth. It could mean increased collectivity among bookstores—the threats outlined in this book are certainly big enough to warrant more collective action. Of course, it could also mean collective action by booksellers to improve

the dignity of their work. Maybe the answer isn't
independence but rather interdependence.

Some of these ideas are pie in the sky, admittedly, but I do believe
it's worth it to write them down. In *Chokepoint Capitalism*, Cory
Doctorow and Rebecca Giblin write, "You never know what
might happen to the ideas you have laying around."[79] And the
idea of systematic support for bookstores, based on the value
they bring their communities, isn't impossible. We already
have examples to show that investment in bookstores is worth
it. Source Booksellers expanded thanks to grant support from
Midtown Detroit, Inc., and the Book Industry Charitable
Foundation. Red Emma's bought their building thanks to
a loaded roster of community organizations committed to
the same ideals that the bookstore café has held for almost
two decades. In Canada, the government is engaged in an
extended project to bolster Canadian publishers, writers, and
now bookstores, an effort which Biblioasis has felt in multiple
ways. And the French government has made a series of policy
decisions with the explicit intent of supporting bookstores
and preventing Amazon from encroaching on their market,
allowing a haven like Shakespeare and Company to flourish for
many decades. I dream big because there's already evidence that
external, systematic support for bookstores can work.

Throughout this book, and all my activism, I'm hesitant to
pin too much responsibility on you, reader, since these systemic
issues aren't your fault (unless you happen to be Robert Bork or
Ronald Reagan). The people who are invested in maintaining
the systems that make it so hard for bookstores might even see
it to their advantage if people blame themselves for the failure
of those systems. But even though many of the solutions to
the obstacles bookstores face are systemic, there's still a lot an
individual can do. I'd argue that the best thing you can do, right
now, right here, after you put this book down, is to take steps
to make sure you're a regular and devoted member of your

bookstore's community. As Loyalty Bookstores' Hannah Oliver Depp told me when I asked them what people can do: "Show up." Buy books, sure, but it doesn't stop there. Wander the stacks. Go to events. Bring your kids. If the right-wingers try to rob your bookstore of its right to create an inclusive environment for kids and their families, show up as a counterprotestor. There's a lot of work to be done, but the first step is to simply make yourself a part of your bookstore's story. You will be a better reader and community member for it, and you'll be doing your small part to make sure that story is a long one.

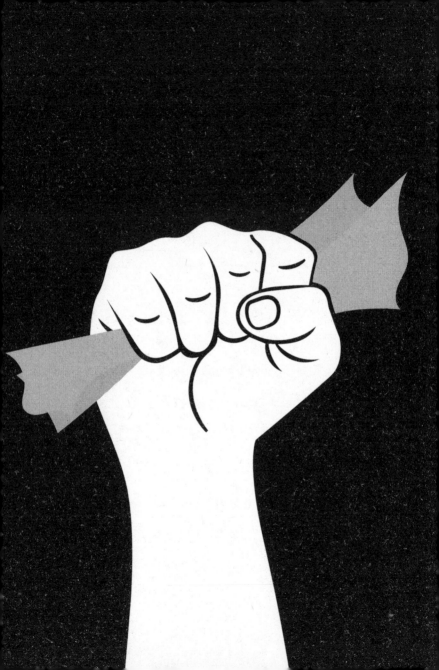

# ACKNOWLEDGEMENTS

My first thanks must go to all the wonderful booksellers who talked to me for this project, giving me invaluable insight into their stories and trusting me to tell them: Nina Barrett, Adam Biles, Luis Correa, Laura De Heredia, Hannah Oliver Depp, Louise Erdrich, Linda Fallon, Janet Geddis, Janet Webster Jones, Sara Luce Look, Gary Lovely, Lynn Mooney, Danni Mullen, Cullen Nawalkowsky, Eric Obenauf, Christine Onorati, Angela Schwesnedl, Gretchen Treu, Alyson Jones Turner, Rachel Watkins, Dan Wells, and Sylvia Whitman. Your hospitality and willingness to share your stories and knowledge are what made this project possible. Thanks also to Allison Hill and Dan Cullen for answering my nitty-gritty book industry questions. Thank you to the EIBF and RISE Bookselling for funding my trip to Europe, without which the Shakespeare and Company chapter wouldn't be possible. Thank you to Shakespeare and Company for hosting me as a writer in residence; it let me finish this book in high style. Thank you also to the team at Microcosm, including but not limited to Joe, Elly, and Olivia, as well as Drew and all the other warehouse folks—I'm forever grateful to you for letting me write the book I wanted to write, helping me shape it into the book you're now holding, and getting it into the hands of readers. Thank you to the writing group of Michelle Malonzo and Angela Maria Spring for your support and guidance in the early stages of writing this book. Thanks as always to PBR Writers Club—Althea, Chance, Julia, Maggie, Rachel, and Will—for the companionship, feedback, and snacks. Thank you to Ada Calhoun for the excellent advice about conducting live interviews. Thank you to the entire team of Raven booksellers—Adela, Chris, Christina, Jack, Kahill, Kami, Kelly, Lily, Manda, Mary, Miranda, Nancy, Nikita, Sameah, Sarah, and Wulfe—for helping to show me what a bookstore can do, and for being the best bunch of booksellers in the universe. And as always, thank you to my parents, and to Kara and Jack for the never-ending support.

# REFERENCES

1 American Booksellers Association and Civic Economics, *Unfulfilled: Amazon and the American Retail Landscape* (2022), 4.

2 ABA and Civic Economics, *Unfulfilled*, 4.

3 Chris Gregory, Regine Sonderland Saga, and Cathy Parker. *Booksellers as Placemakers: The Contribution of Booksellers to the Vitality and Viability of High Streets* (Institute of Place Management, 2022).

4 Gregory, Sonderland Saga, and Parker, *Booksellers as Placemakers*, 7.

5 Jeff Deutsch, *In Praise of Good Bookstores* (Princeton: Princeton University Press, 2022), 79.

6 Deutsch, *Good Bookstores*, 90.

7 Kimberly Kinder, *The Radical Bookstore: Counterspace for Social Movements* (Minneapolis: University of Minnesota Press, 2021), 6.

8 Kinder, *Radical Bookstore*, 3.

9 Kinder, *Radical Bookstore*, 4.

10 Kim Kelly, "Bookstore Workers Are Forming Unions Over Low Pay and Lack of Benefits," *Teen Vogue*, May 5, 2022, teenvogue.com/story/bookstore-workers-union.

11 Alexandra Alter and Elizabeth A. Harris, "Some Surprising Good News: Bookstores Are Booming and Becoming More Diverse," *New York Times*, July 10, 2022, nytimes.com/2022/07/10/books/bookstores-diversity-pandemic.html.

12 Gary Rivlin, *Saving Main Street* (New York: HarperCollins, 2022), 10.

13 Brendan Farrington, "DeSantis Signs Bill Targeting Explicit Books in Schools," *Associated Press*, March 25, 2022, apnews.com/article/entertainment-florida-ron-desantis-school-boards-libraries-da50c-9c4091868e121484425d290385b.

14 Laura J. Miller, *Reluctant Capitalists: Bookselling and the Culture of Consumption* (Chicago: University of Chicago Press, 2007), 163.

15 Miller, *Reluctant Capitalists*, 162.

16 Miller, *Reluctant Capitalists*, 161, 163.

17 Miller, *Reluctant Capitalists*, 164.

18 Jenny Gross, "Curbside Pickup. Bicycle Deliveries. Virtual Book Discussions. Amid Virus, Bookstores Get Creative," *New York Times*,

March 17, 2020, nytimes.com/2020/03/17/us/independent-bookstores-coronavirus.html.

19  Louise Erdrich, *Books and Islands in Ojibwe Country: Traveling through the Land of My Ancestors* (New York: Harper Perennial, 2003), 116.

20  Erdrich, *Books and Islands*, 114.

21  Erdrich, *Books and Islands*, 117.

22  Deutsch, *Good Bookstores*, 24.

23  Diane Dragan, "10 Outrageous Markups You'd Never Guess You Were Paying," RD.com, March 16, 2022, rd.com/list/10-outrageous-markups-youd-never-guess-you-were-paying/.

24  Rachel Mipro, "Future of Kansas Town's Library in Jeopardy over Refusal to Remove 'Divisive' Books," *Kansas Reflector*, November 14, 2022, kansasreflector.com/2022/11/14/future-of-kansas-towns-library-in-jeopardy-over-refusal-to-remove-divisive-books/.

25  Mipro, "Future of Kansas."

26  Rachel Mipro, "Kansas Town's Library Lease Renewed after Months of Debate about LGBTQ Content." *Kansas Reflector*, December 7, 2022, kansasreflector.com/2022/12/06/kansas-towns-library-lease-renewed-after-months-of-debate-about-lgbtq-content/.

27  Kristen Hogan, *The Feminist Bookstore Movement: Lesbian Antiracism and Feminist Accountability* (Durham: Duke University Press, 2016), XIX.

28  Hogan, *Feminist Bookstore Movement*, 3.

29  Hogan, *Feminist Bookstore Movement*, 3.

30  Hogan, *Feminist Bookstore Movement*, 177.

31  Claire Kirch, "Bookselling Profile: A Room of One's Own," *Publishers Weekly*, June 11, 2021, publishersweekly.com/pw/by-topic/industry-news/bookselling/article/86640-bookselling-profile-a-room-of-one-s-own.html.

32  Hogan, *Feminist Bookstore Movement*, XV.

33  Hogan, *Feminist Bookstore Movement*, 109.

34  Carrie Obry, "A Room of One's Own Celebrated with the Midwest Bookseller of the Year Award," Midwest Independent Booksellers Association, October 4, 2021, midwestbooksellers.org/news/staff-at-room-of-ones-own-granted-midwest-bookseller-of-the-year-award/.

35  Ed Nawotka, "Wisconsin Booksellers Win PW Star Watch Award," *Publishers Weekly*, November 17, 2021, publishersweekly.com/pw/by-topic/

industry-news/awards-and-prizes/article/87910-wisconsin-booksellers-win-pw-s-star-watch-award.html.

36  Hogan, *Feminist Bookstore Movement*, 143.

37  Josh Cook, *Tell Me Everything You've Ever Thought and Felt in Thirty Seconds: On Connection, Intuition, and the Art of Handselling* (Windsor: Biblioasis, 2023), 15.

38  Edward Lempinen, "A $15 Minimum Wage Would Cost Jobs, Right? Probably Not, Economists Say," *Berkeley News*, March 18, 2021, news.berkeley.edu/2021/03/18/a-15-minimum-wage-would-cost-jobs-right-probably-not-economists-say/.

39  Krista Halverson, ed., *Shakespeare and Company, Paris: A History of the Rag & Bone Shop of the Heart* (Paris: Shakespeare and Company, 2016), 42.

40  Halverson, *Shakespeare and Company*, 184.

41  Halverson, *Shakespeare and Company*, 172.

42  Halverson, *Shakespeare and Company*, 186.

43  Halverson, *Shakespeare and Company*, 81.

44  "Chicago Area Independent Bookstores," Chicago Literary Hall of Fame. 2022. chicagoliteraryhof.org/resources/bookstores.

45  Philippine Ramognino, "Commerce en ligne: se faire livrer un livre coûtera bientôt 3 euros," *Le Parisien*, April 10, 2023, leparisien.fr/economie/consommation/commerce-en-ligne-se-faire-livrer-un-livre-coutera-bientot-3-euros-10-04-2023-2TKY5ELXKNHXFAQ2W6RM62CXOA.php.

46  Phillippine Ramognino, "Commerce en ligne."

47  Halverson, ed., *Shakespeare and Company*, 254.

48  Rochelle Valverde, "Historic Preservation Board Says Proposed Apartment Project Inappropriate for Downtown," *Lawrence Journal-World*, March 21, 2019, www2.ljworld.com/news/city-government/2019/mar/21/historic-preservation-board-says-proposed-apartment-project-inappropriate-for-downtown/.

49  Kinder, *Radical Bookstore*, 52.

50  Kinder, *Radical Bookstore*, 52.

51  Kinder, *Radical Bookstore*, 52.

52  Kinder, *Radical Bookstore*, 50.

53  Christina Tkacik, "Baltimore's Red Emma's Is Moving Again, This Time to a 'Forever Home' of Its Own in Waverly," *The Baltimore Sun*,

April 23, 2021, baltimoresun.com/food-drink/bs-fo-red-emmas-moves-20210423-vz67fie5ezfvhczwn4t6pg4xtm-story.html.

54  Kinder, *Radical Bookstore*, 52.

55  Nick Niedzwiadek, "Michigan Strikes Right-to-Work Law Detested by Unions," *Politico*, March 24, 2023, politico.com/news/2023/03/24/michigan-strikes-right-to-work-law-00088762.

56  Claire Woodcock, "Striking Workers Just Won a Historic Union Contract at Book Giant HarperCollins," *Motherboard: Tech by Vice*, February 17, 2023, vice.com/en/article/wxnwe4/striking-workers-just-won-historic-union-contract-harpercollins.

57  Kelly, "Bookstore Workers."

58  Kelly, "Bookstore Workers."

59  Juozas Kaziukenas, "Amazon Takes a 50% Cut of Seller's Revenue," *Marketplace Pulse*, February 13, 2023, marketplacepulse.com/articles/amazon-takes-a-50-cut-of-sellers-revenue.

60  Victoria Bisset, "Judge Blocks Simon & Schuster and Penguin Random House Merger," *Washington Post*, November 1, 2022, washingtonpost.com/business/2022/11/01/penguin-random-house-simon-schuster-merger-blocked/.

61  Stacy Mitchell and Reggie Rucker, "'The Beginning of the End of the Consumer Welfare Standard,' Stacy Mitchell Says of Blocked Merger of Penguin Random House and Simon & Schuster," Institute for Local Self-Reliance, November 1, 2022, ilsr.org/statement-penguin-random-house-simon-schuster-merger-blocked/.

62  Victoria Bekiempis, "Judge Shuts Book on Penguin Random House–Simon & Schuster Merger," *Vulture*, November 1, 2022, vulture.com/2022/11/judge-blocks-prh-simon-schuster-merger.html.

63  Cory Doctorow, "We Need to Talk about Audible," *Publishers Weekly*, September 18, 2020, publishersweekly.com/pw/by-topic/industry-news/libraries/article/84384-we-need-to-talk-about-audible.html.

64  Rebecca Giblin and Cory Doctorow, *Chokepoint Capitalism* (New York: Beacon Press, 2022), 27.

65  Giblin and Doctorow, *Chokepoint Capitalism*, 24.

66  Giblin and Doctorow, *Chokepoint Capitalism*, 31.

67  Quinn Myers, "Wicker Park's Semicolon Bookstore Moving Back to River West After Owner Gets Chance to Buy Property," *Block Club Chicago*, December 5, 2022, blockclubchicago.org/2022/12/05/wicker-parks-semicolon-bookstore-moving-back-to-river-west-after-owner-gets-chance-to-buy-property/#:~:text=Bucktown%2C%20West%20Town-

,Wicker%20Park's%20Semicolon%20Bookstore%20Moving%20Back%20
To%20River%20West%20After,Halsted%20St.

68  Robin Andersen, "The 'Copaganda' Epidemic: How Media Glori-
fies Police and Vilifies Protestors," Salon.com, January 8, 2023, salon.
com/2023/01/08/the-copaganda-epidemic-how-media-glorifies-police-
and-vilifies/.

69  Brandon Soderberg and Andy Friedman, "Major Media Outlets
Can't Stop Describing Police Violence as 'Officer-Involved' Incidents,"
*HuffPost*, January 13, 2022, HuffPost.com/entry/police-violence-officer-
involved-analysis-lapd_n_61df310fe4b0a26702885448.

70  Giblin and Doctorow, *Chokepoint Capitalism*, 40.

71  ABA and Civic Economics, *Unfulfilled*, 10.

72  Jason Guriel, *On Browsing* (Windsor: Biblioasis, 2022), 52.

73  Emma Wager, Jared Ortaliza, and Cynthia Cox, "How Does Health
Spending in the U.S. Compare to Other Countries?" Health System
Tracker, January 1, 2022, healthsystemtracker.org/chart-collection/
health-spending-u-s-compare-countries-2/#GDP%20per%20capita%20
and%20health%20consumption%20spending%20per%20capita,%20
2020%20(U.S.%20dollars,%20PPP%20adjusted).

74  Annie McDonough, "NYPD, Other Uniformed Agency Overtime
Spending Is on the Rise," *City & State NY*, August 17, 2022, cityandstateny.
com/policy/2022/08/nypd-other-uniformed-agency-overtime-spending-
rise/375996/.

75  GLAAD, "UPDATED Report: Drag Events Faced More than 160
Protests and Significant Threats Since Early 2022," GLAAD.org, glaad.
org/blog/anti-drag-report.

76  Ginny Bixby, "Protest at Drag Story Hour in Silver Spring
Turns Violent, Witnesses Say," *MoCo360*, February 19, 2023, moco360.
media/2023/02/19/protest-at-drag-story-hour-in-silver-spring-turns-
violent-witnesses-say/.

77  Giblin and Doctorow, *Chokepoint Capitalism*, 146.

78  Nina Raemont, "Black Garnet Books Builds Inclusion into Its St.
Paul Bookstore," *Streets MN*, February 22, 2023, streets.mn/2023/02/22/
black-garnet-books/.

79  Giblin and Doctorow, *Chokepoint Capitalism*, 153.

# ABOUT THE AUTHOR

Danny Caine is the author of the poetry collections *Continental Breakfast, El Dorado Freddy's, Flavortown,* and *Picture Window,* as well as the book *How to Resist Amazon and Why.* His poetry has appeared in *The Slowdown, DIAGRAM, HAD,* and *Barrelhouse,* and his prose has appeared in *Literary Hub* and *Publishers Weekly.* In 2019, he received the Midwest Independent Booksellers Association Midwest Bookseller of the Year Award. He's a co-owner of the Raven Book Store, *Publishers Weekly*'s 2022 bookstore of the year. More at dannycaine.com.